Pathways to Self-Determination

Canadian Indians and the Canadian State

edited by

Leroy Little Bear

Menno Boldt

J. Anthony Long

UNIVERSITY OF TORONTO PRESS

Toronto Buffalo London

© University of Toronto Press 1984
Toronto Buffalo London
Printed in Canada
Reprinted 1985, 1986

ISBN 0-8020-2524-2 – cloth
ISBN 0-8020-6539-2 – paper

Canadian Cataloguing in Publication Data
Main entry under title:
Pathways to self-determination

ISBN 0-8020-2524-2 (bound). – ISBN 0-8020-6539-2 (pbk.)

1. Indians of North America – Canada – Government
relations – Addresses, essays, lectures. 2. Indians
of North America – Canada – Legal status, laws, etc. –
Addresses, essays, lectures. 3. Indians, Treatment of
– Canada – Addresses, essays, lectures. I. Little Bear,
Leroy. II. Boldt, Menno, 1930-   III. Long, J.
Anthony.

E92.P37   323.1'197'071   C83-098739-8

Publication of this book has been assisted by the
Canada Council and the Ontario Arts Council
under their block-grant programs.

Contents

Preface

The initial stimulus for this book came from our awareness that the Indian perspective is largely missing from published materials on issues affecting Indians. Although the past decade has witnessed a significant growth in the literature about Indians, very few of the works comprising that literature are by Indians. This is not to detract from the existing body of literature. Indeed, non-Indian historians, anthropologists, sociologists, and journalists have given us valid, replicable observations and insights about what is happening with Indians. Enlightened non-Indian social scientists and others have written empathetically about the Indian condition and have advocated more effective Indian policies. But they have done so from the perspective of outsiders. Evidence of the outsider perspective is manifest in the pervasive European–Western liberal conceptualization of Indian rights and goals. This ideology finds expression in an uncritical acceptance of political and social institutions for Indians that are based on the doctrine of individualism. Such an ideology is markedly at variance with the traditional Indian concept of collective rights and rule by consensus.

Understandably, Indians resent and object to what they perceive as academic paternalism and an assimilationist bias in much of the literature on Indian issues and policies. They hold that no one can know as much as Indians themselves about what policies are valid for them and that any analysis of Indian issues that ignores or neglects a systematic exploration of Indian viewpoints inspires suspicion. The Indian perspective must be heard and acknowledged for a meaningful dialogue to occur between Indians and non-Indians.

This anthology began at a conference on Indian government held at the University of Lethbridge in the spring of 1981. Its special purpose is to present the perspective of Indians on the topic of government for status Indians. For this we have drawn heavily on the views of Indian people. Most of the contributors are Indian leaders, who speak from personal experiences in their struggle to achieve meaningful self-determination for their people. Recognizing that Indians do not speak with one voice, we have sought a cross-section of viewpoints, taking into consideration tribal, geographical, and organizational diversities.

In assembling this anthology we have become aware of the need to hear the Indian point of view on other key issues of concern to them. These include aboriginal rights, treaty rights, and Indian-provincial relationships. It is our hope that this volume will be the beginning of a series of systematic efforts to develop and disseminate the Indian perspective on such issues of central concern.

We are indebted to many others who have contributed to or assisted in the preparation of this volume. A special thanks is due those whose works are published here; with only two exceptions all of the pieces were prepared especially for this collection. Several persons provided valuable secretarial and clerical assistance in the preparation of the manuscripts; in this regard we wish to acknowledge the assistance of Marg McKeen, Carol Tomomitsu, Lana Cooke, Liz Zorzetti, and Diane Bennett. We wish also to thank R.I.K. Davidson for his careful evaluation of and suggestions for the book. Finally, we want to acknowledge the financial assistance of the Muttart Foundation and the Department of Native American Studies, University of Lethbridge, Alberta.

Introduction

Prior to European colonization Indians of North America were independent, self-governing nations. Under British colonial tutelage, however, the authority of Indian government was gradually eroded. Using the pretext of 'protecting' Indians, the British systematically usurped Indian authority. This policy of diminishing Indian independence and their capacity to govern themselves was continued by the Canadian government when it assumed responsibility from the British for discharging the provisions of the Indian treaties. Under the British North America Act of 1867 and the Indian Act of 1876, the Canadian minister responsible for Indian affairs exercised total control over Indians and their lands.

The objective of Canada's Indian policy from the beginning was to 'civilize' (meaning 'assimilate') and integrate Indians, by degrees, into Canadian social, economic, and political structures. Traditional tribal government was seen as an obstacle to this process of civilization and integration. Thus, Canadian Indian policy called for the elimination of all vestiges of indigenous political institutions. One of the Canadian government's initial steps upon assuming responsibility for Indian affairs from the British was to replace traditional tribal political institutions with so-called 'democratic' elective systems. This was done to prepare Indians for municipal types of institutions, like those of other Canadians. It was contemplated that the elected band councils would ultimately 'graduate' to the level of exercising the same powers as municipal councils. Thus, the Canadian government would achieve greater control over Indians, and, at the same time, Indians would become part and parcel of the Canadian political system.

The first legislative provisions for an elective Indian government appeared in the 1876 Indian Act. This act conferred the 'privilege' on 'advanced' (advanced, that is, 'in intelligence and civilization') Indian bands to request an elected band-council system in place of existing traditional systems of Indian government. Under the act, elected band councils had only very limited powers to make regulations. Any financial decisions, for example, required the approval of the Canadian government minister responsible for Indian Affairs. All band-council legislation had to conform to the Indian Act, and the minister had veto powers over all band-council enactments. In effect, under the elective system the minister and his executive arm, the Indian Affairs Branch, totally controlled almost every aspect of Indian life: education, law enforcement, agriculture, commerce, health, welfare, housing, employment, and so on. In practice the Branch pretended to be generous with self-government when Indian councils acted consistently with Branch objectives, but it was very restrictive when they acted in conflict with Branch policies and goals.

The electoral provisions of the 1876 Indian Act met with very broadly based resistance among Indian tribes, which were committed to their traditional system of tribal government. The election provisions of the act were developed without any reference to previous tribal systems of government, and they were implemented with little sensitivity to traditional values. Elected governments were viewed as alien in form and function. Most Indians recognized the intent of the act – that is, to assimilate Indians by subverting their traditional political institutions. This perception was given credence by provisions in the act that deliberately encouraged *individual* property rights and landholdings on reserve lands. Whereas the traditional Indian concept of government relied on consensus, the elective system, with its hierarchical authority structure and majority rule, encouraged factionalism. Many Indian tribes were divided into 'traditionalists' on the one side and, on the other, those who saw in the elective system an opportunity to exercise personal power. The latter faction were often aided and abetted in their designs by local Branch personnel and by the clergy, who viewed the traditional institutions as a hindrance to their objectives.

Since the 1876 Indian Act came into force, Indian bands have progressively accepted the electoral provisions of the Act. However, this is not to be interpreted as a voluntary action. Acceptance represents a concession to harsh reality. At the time the electoral provisions were being introduced, tribal government had already been rendered completely powerless. The electoral provisions thus were held out by the Canadian government as the instrument whereby Indians could increase, if not restore, their former powers of self-government. This deception doomed traditional Indian government because elected government now came to be seen as the only way to survival. But elected band governments were never allowed to act as tribal governments; they served merely as administrative structures for implementing the approved policies and regulations of the Canadian government. In effect, band councils functioned as agents of the Canadian government in a model of colonial indirect rule rather than as representatives responsible to their own people.

Historically, under the provisions of the BNA Act and the Indian Act, Indians have had a very strong relationship with the federal government and a very weak relationship with the provincial governments. Currently, the federal government through the Indian Affairs Branch provides Indians with a complex of services that other Canadians receive from provincial or local governments. Although the Constitution permits the provincial governments to extend any services to Indians that the federal government allows (and the federal government has been extremely permissive in this regard), all provinces are uniformly reluctant to accept financial responsibility for services to Indians within their boundaries. In part this explains why Indian bands are still outside the bulk of provincial programs.

That Indians do not have access to provincial and local services as do other Canadians has been a long-standing concern of the federal government. In recent times, the federal government has moved to change this situation. For example, the federal government has insisted that federally supported and provincially administered programs, such as medicare, must include Indians. Negotiations between the federal government and provincial authorities have also produced arrangements under which Indians can enrol in the regular provincial school system. However, there is a serious flaw in such arrangements: on-reserve Indians are legally prohibited by legislation from being elected to sit on local or provincial legislative bodies.

Indians have been very reluctant to accept services and assistance from provincial governments. They see in the federal government's move to integrate Indian bands into the provincial-municipal structure much more than a simple extension of provincial services. They interpret it as part of the federal government's hidden agenda to abrogate its constitutional and treaty obligations to the Indian people. They view a transfer of dependency from the federal government to ten provincial governments as the death sentence for their historical claim to nationhood and self-government. Furthermore, they reject the assertion that a transfer of dependency will produce an improvement in their life-condition. They cite as evidence the case of the Métis people of Indian ancestry, who legally are full provincial citizens yet whose plight is more deplorable than that of status Indians.

Indian leaders lay claim to sovereignty and nationhood for their people. Their conception of sovereignty and nationhood, with some variations, usually includes ideas of self-government, autonomous institutions, a territorial land base, and a resource base so that they can maintain the integrity of their culture and society. They want exclusive legislative rights in their territories. They hold that their right to self-government is an inherent right derived from the Creator, who gave that authority to all the Indian people. They point out that this is a right that pre-dates the Canadian government; thus, the Canadian government was never in a position to create or grant Indian self-government but merely to acknowledge it. They assert, furthermore, that their inherent and historical right to self-government was explicitly recognized by the Crown in the treaty agreements with Indians. Therefore, any power exercised by the Canadian government over Indians, unless it has been freely delegated by Indians, is illegal.

The Canadian government's position is quite different. It holds that Indians possess and can exercise only those powers that are bestowed on them by Parliament. In the Canadian government's view, Indians are subject to the laws of Canada, and their right to self-government, if any, is a delegated and limited privilege. This position has been consistently upheld in judicial decisions by Canadian courts. The concept of a sovereign Indian nation is anathema to the Canadian government, which has uniformly insisted on limiting any negotiations on Indian government to discussions of increased band-level administrative powers on Indian reserves. This is to be achieved through a devolution of powers from the minister of Indian Affairs to the elected band council, but with ultimate control continuing to be vested in the Canadian government.

Although Canadian governments and courts have consistently ruled that Indians are subordinate to Parliament, Indian claims to nationhood and sovereignty have historical and moral justification. At the time of first European contact they existed as independent, self-governing nations or tribes; they exercised effective control over geographical areas; and they traded and made war with other nations. Indian leaders point out that their forefathers never surrendered their nationhood or right to self-government, nor was it taken from them by conquest. They claim that these rights were usurped surreptitiously by successive British and Canadian governments, in contravention of international law. The refusal by the Canadian government, until recently, to grant Indians full rights of Canadian citizenship is interpreted by Indians as clear evidence that Indians held another kind of citizenship.

The Indians' sense of their own nationhood derives also from having their own language and culture and from a conscious knowledge of shared tribal achievements and glories in their past. This Indian sense of historical nationhood has its roots in British colonial policy. Specifically, it was fostered by the signing of treaties and the British tendency to segregate their colonial wards legally, administratively, and socially. Whereas the French colonizers were inclined to assimilate their colonial subjects into the mother country, stopping not even at intermarriage, the British rarely mingled socially with their colonial subjects, and the 'arms-length' colonial policy of the British contributed to the survival of traditional Indian political, economic, and socio-cultural institutions. When Canada assumed responsibility for the Indians, the essential elements of the British colonial style were maintained; hence, despite the official policy of cultural assimilation, the Canadian government's practice of virtually excluding Indians from the rest of Canadian society by geographical segregation and by administration under a separate act has helped to preserve their self-identity.

The Indian's continuing sense of nationhood is further fostered by the fact that they are significantly unlike other Canadian ethnic groups. They alone have an inalienable land base, aboriginal and treaty rights, and a special status in the Constitution and the Royal Proclamation. Also unlike all others living in the Americas, they are not immigrants. They are the original people; they have no other homeland.

Indians have little expectation that their situation will improve in the context of Canadian political, economic, and socio-cultural structures.

But far from wanting to give up their special status to achieve justice and equal treatment, Indians are convinced that their special status needs to be fortified by self-government for them to achieve their vision of 'the good society.' Thus, they advocate a concept of Indian government as a distinct order of government, a concept that the Iroquois express in symbolic terms as the 'two-row wampum belt,' signifying the parallel and equal arrangement of Indian and white societies.

Self-government is seen by Indians as necessary to preserve their philosophical uniqueness. They seek self-government so that they can develop their own institutions and shape laws to reflect and enhance their traditional cultural values. They do not want merely a European-Western model of government that is run by Indians; rather, they want an Indian government that operates in accordance with traditional principles and customs, one that rests on a spiritual base and emphasizes group, not individual, rights. They want a government that will restore their relationship with the natural environment rather than try to assimilate them into the dominant society.

The immediate goal of Indian leaders is to enhance significantly the governing powers of local band councils. These efforts to enlarge local autonomy are not unlike the steps to independence that have been taken by the newly emerged nations – that is, a gradual increase in the participation of the people in the administration of their affairs, with the ultimate objective being full control over their own political, economic, and socio-cultural institutions. Evidence that Indians are on such a quest can be observed in the development of an Indian press and in the moves to assume responsibility for law and order in their communities and for the administration of their reserves.

Although aboriginal land claims and the irrevocable rights to reservations are crucial concerns for Indians, their concept of self-government and nationhood is not exclusively geographically based. Because the reserves cannot support all of their people, the significant boundaries of nationhood and self-government for Indians are defined in terms of political, economic, and socio-cultural criteria. Indians are asking for a special status for their people, whether on the reserve or off. They are asking for a relationship to the Canadian government that will give them, *as a group*, political, economic, and socio-cultural equality with the rest of Canadian society while allowing them to retain their identity as

Indians. They want this status not as a privilege bestowed by a benevolent Canadian government, nor as a concession from a fashionably 'liberal' society; they want this status recognized as their inherent right.
They understand very well that self-government implies certain essential
requisites, such as an adequate land base and economic self-sufficiency.
They hold that, under the treaties, the government of Canada is obligated
to provide the essential requisites that will enable them to achieve a
meaningful level of self-determination.

There still exist considerable differences among Indians over how best
to advance their goals of self-government and nationhood. For example,
there is still no consensus among them as to the wisdom of using their
federal and provincial voting rights. While some view the right to vote in
federal and provincial elections as a means to effect desired changes,
many consider the Canadian government's offer of citizenship and the
right to vote as a stratagem for undermining Indian claims to separate
nationhood. Similarly, there is no consensus about the future of the
Indian Affairs Branch. Despite its odious past, many Indians oppose its
elimination. They propose instead that the Branch be staffed and operated by Indians. It would continue to function, in order to fulfil the
Canadian government's treaty obligations.

Recently, the combined effect of increased contact with white society
and the Canadian policy of forced acculturation has served to heighten
Indians' perceptions that they, *collectively* as Indians – that is, without
tribal distinctions – are victims of injustice and inequities.

Indian leaders today are groping for new relationships among their
tribally based Indian communities that will provide a framework for
provincial and national political unity. The idea of Indian political coalition is not new. In the past this pattern has occurred in the formation of
loose regional confederacies; the Iroquois League of Six Nations is probably the best-known example. Until recently, however, there have been
no attempts to organize tribes through unifying political organizations
and symbols into a single *national* force. Yet today we observe a promi-
nent pan-Indian trend that transcends intertribal rivalry and suspicions.
Canadian Indians are showing an effective capacity for restraint and
compromise in forging a single pan-Indian political society. They are
transferring some of their tribal loyalty to the larger community of Indians. Evidence of this new attitude can be observed not only in the cur-

rently functioning provincial and national Indian associations but also in the forceful insistence throughout the community that *Indians* – without tribal connotation – participate in decisions that concern them.

The unifying sense of commonality and community expressed in the pan-Indian movement has its origins in the universal Indian experience of discrimination and of being deprived of treaty and aboriginal rights. This shared experience provides not only a basis for transcending tribal identifications; it also furnishes a viable framework within which leaders from various Indian tribes can formulate mutually acceptable goals. But pan-Indianism is not merely a reactive movement. It is also an expression of a deep appreciation by Indians for their own positive qualities and values. It grows out of their conceptions of the type of society they would like to build.

Although the Canadian government is opposed to Indian unity, it has, ironically, provided both means and motive for pan-Indian unity. Such unity would have been immeasurably more difficult, if not impossible, had the Canadian government not undermined or destroyed many of the traditional political and social institutions, thereby facilitating new intertribal relationships. Then too, compulsory education of Indians provided a shared language and the skills to utilize modern means of communication. The electoral provisions of the Indian Act gave Indians the opportunity to gain political and bureaucratic experience. All of these conditions together encouraged the interest in organizational techniques that enabled Indians to build the integrative institutions necessary to develop and maintain a unified political strategy. The motive for such a movement emerged from the Canadian government's policy of excluding Indians from political, economic, and socio-cultural participation in Canadian life while, at the same time, controlling every aspect of their lives.

While pan-Indian political organizations currently function on both the national and provincial levels, the role of these political organizations typically has been to lobby on behalf of Indian interests but not to govern. At present, only local band councils have a legislative base under the Indian Act, and band councils are loath to delegate significant powers to provincial and national Indian organizations. The idea of delegating significant powers to provincial and national Indian organizations is more attractive to the weaker and poorer tribes than it is to the stronger and more prosperous ones: the 'have' bands believe they may have to give up more than they will gain as participants in a united political front. With both the Canadian government and local band councils reluctant to delegate governing powers to pan-Indian organizations and given the uneven distribution of wealth, the cultural diversity, the geographic dispersion, and the legal divisions of Indian constituencies, it is unlikely that pan-Indian government will soon be realized. Although the call for Indian self-government is emerging as a pan-Indian aspiration, when one considers the present level of development of Indian institutional structures, attitudinal support, and legal legitimacy, the aspiration for self-government has its greatest potential for realization at the local band level.

In its 1969 White Paper the Canadian government reasserted in explicit terms its historical policy of termination and assimilation of Indians. It proposed to extend to Indians the right of full and equal participation in the political, economic, and social life of Canada. The goal was to treat Indians as any other ethnic group within a common multicultural policy. This policy objective was to be achieved by repealing the Indian Act and removing the special status of Indians under the BNA Act. Clearly, the Indian Act, by providing the legislative base for Canadian government control over Indians, represents a serious obstacle to Indian aspirations to self-government. But, while Indians resent the Indian Act and want to end their state of colonial dependence under it, they adamantly and vehemently resist all moves by the federal government to repeal or modify the Act without constitutional guarantees for their treaty and aboriginal rights. They suspect that the Canadian government's interest in changing or eliminating the Act has more to do with its desire to extricate itself from costly treaty obligations than it has with the proclaimed concern to decolonize Indians.

Beyond the thorny problem of differences between what Indians see as an acceptable level of self-governing powers and what the federal and provincial governments are willing to concede, there lie other impediments to Indian political independence. If Indians want their government to act independently, then they must reduce their current state of economic dependence on the federal government. Yet Indian culture (the complex of institutions, values, and ways of doing things) in its present configuration is not conducive to capitalistic notions of economic development. The system of economic and social-emotional security that prevails on the reserves is still based substantially on reciprocal obligations within the kinship group. The prospering Indian individual must be prepared to share his goods with less fortunate kinfolk. This aspect of the kinfolk or tribal system has the effect of discouraging accumulation of capital as well as dampening individual ambition. Thus, it would seem that Indian culture represents an obstacle to Indian aspirations to meaningful self-government.

The promise of a better life is being used by Indian leaders to generate broad support for the Indian self-government movement. But the prospects that Indian self-government will be able to provide a better life are dim. The extent of reserved land under present treaties is relatively fixed, while the Indian population is increasing sharply. European-Western society has adjusted to population increase through urbanization, but such an option offers opportunities for only a few Indians. Unless Indians can achieve a great leap forward in economic development on their reserves – an unlikely prospect – the limit of the reserves' capacity to support their populations will soon be reached and they will be confronted with two options: to move off the reserve and become assimilated to Canadian society or to become increasingly dependent on the Canadian government's welfare programs. The absence of economic development in the reserves presents a very real obstacle for any Indian hopes to improve their condition through increased political autonomy.

Perhaps the most important variable in the evolution of Indian self-government is political leadership. Wise and experienced leadership is critical, not only for negotiating a new political relationship with the Canadian state but also to help fledgling Indian governments to survive the early stages of their development. One of the problems of Indian leadership arises from the need to come to terms with white society. Attempts by Indian leaders to deal with white society often leave them open to suspicion of playing the Canadian government's game for their own personal advantage and advancement. This dilemma is not easily resolved, and, if it results in a high turnover of leadership, the consequences will be an insecure, inexperienced, and ineffectual leadership.

Another problem of Indian leadership is that of maintaining sensitivity to the aspirations of all constituents. The growth of administrative units at the local, provincial, and national levels has introduced a hierarchical structure with status differences and greater separation between leaders and rank-and-file members, inhibiting members from participation in decision-making. In short, traditional 'Indian democracy' has become unworkable. Furthermore, the shortage of trained Indians enhances the authority of those with expertise, especially as the need for administrative specialists grows. As local, provincial, and national Indian councils assume greater responsibilities for an increasing number of public services, these new administrative structures open the door to abuse of power. There is evidence, for example, at the local level that some band councils become dominated by cliques or kin groups. This leads to insensitivity to the grievances of non-kin constituents and intolerance of opposition. Should this tendency to factionalism extend to the provincial or national Indian organizations, it could result in mass disaffection with the Indian government movement.

Indian leaders are gaining experience in the skills of communication with the alienated and in dealing with white authority. But skills in the political techniques of attaining autonomy are quite different from the art of administration. Indian leaders, in order to maintain their credibility as leaders, must articulate policies that satisfy the aspirations of their people; one effect of the leaders' response, however, is that Canadian Indians develop expectations that run ahead of the system's capacity to deliver. Indian people want immediate action to alleviate their deprived condition. The demand for a better life will not diminish with increased autonomy. Thus, the present momentum of Indians' aspirations suggests troubled times ahead. The movement's success in attracting competent, responsible leaders will determine how effectively the problems currently confronting Indian people will be handled. It will also determine whether the emerging political vigour of Indian people will become a positive force or turn radical to the point that it might trigger a white backlash, which could destroy the self-government movement.

The light and the dark in the drawing overleaf symbolize the cultural duality, the contradictions, and the conflicts that native Americans experience in life. Their cultural dilemma extends to the quest for self-government. The drawing portrays the challenge they face in trying to conceptualize new political arrangements that will allow them to survive as a people without compromising their spiritual-cultural heritage.

To be sure, many other meanings may also be read into this drawing which wouldn't be any less true.

The Cree Indian artist ALFRED YOUNG MAN (b 1948) is an assistant professor in the Native American Studies Department of the University of Lethbridge.

1 Cultural and Ideological Foundations

IN THEIR MODEL of self-government, native Indian leaders place great importance on traditional political values and philosophies. Consequently, a recognition and appreciation of those ideas is necessary to an understanding of both the historical roots and the future directions of Indian government. Oren Lyons and Tom Porter, both members of the Iroquois nation, provide penetrating insights into the basic principles governing those traditional political ideas: Oren Lyons places them within the spectrum of contemporary and international ideologies, while Tom Porter locates their foundation and development in the structures of Indian society. Both authors emphasize the non-Western character of traditional Indian thought; both find that significant among its principles is a concept of community, expressed in tribalism, which distinguishes traditional native Indian thought from Western liberalism, with its emphasis on individualism.

Traditionally for the native Indian, involvement with his tribe was integral to his existence as a human being. Ostracism, as Tom Porter points out, was tantamount to a living death. While the individual's inclusion within the wholeness of his tribe was critical to his existence, there still prevailed a respect for individual autonomy and freedom. This is probably best exemplified by the absence in traditional Indian political thought of hierarchical authority, which is integral to Western political and economic organization. Respect for the individual also found expression in decision-making by consensus. Majority rule, as Oren Lyons tells us, only serves to perpetuate factionalism and minority agitation.

Finally, both contributors underscore the importance of spirituality in traditional native political thought. Spirituality was the foundation and the nexus of traditional social and political organization. Through spirituality the natural order of things was revealed and man's proper relationship to nature was established – a relationship of respect and preservation, not exploitation. Spirituality underlies the argument that Indian government has an obligation to maintain the faith for future generations.

It is little wonder that Canada's native Indian peoples resent an externally imposed political order that is highly bureaucratic, secular, and conducive to factionalism.

OREN LYONS

Spirituality, Equality, and Natural Law

The first lesson to be learned when dealing with Indian government is one of patience and one of thoroughness, because there are no short cuts. As soon as you begin to short-cut, you begin to detract from the complete thought and the process for its achievement. This process works through discussion until consensus is reached, not by voting. The problem we have with voting is that you may have more than half the people not agreeing with the decisions of the government. Those who don't agree with the decisions are just going to lie back and wait their chance to get even. Under these circumstances, actions are often taken from a desire to get even rather than on the merits of the action itself. That is why it is important to have a decision-making process whereby you avoid disagreement, and the process Indians advocate is consensus. Consensus involves long discussions, and, if agreement cannot be reached, the issue must be set aside until agreement is possible.

My people, the Iroquois, were very powerful people. They had a coalition of forces that was governed by two fires: the spiritual fire and the political fire. The central fire, of course, was the spiritual fire. The primary law of Indian government is the spiritual law. Spirituality is the highest form of politics, and our spirituality is directly involved in government. As chiefs we are told that our first and most important duty is to see that the spiritual ceremonies are carried out. Without the ceremonies, one does not have a basis on which to conduct government for the welfare of the people. This is not only for our people but for the good of all living things in general. So we are told first to conduct the ceremonies on time, in the proper manner, and then to sit in council for the welfare of our people and of all life.

There is another fundamental understanding in Indian government, and it is that all life is equal. Whether it is the growing life of trees, plants, or animals, or whether it is human, all life is equal. Furthermore, all human beings, black, red, yellow, and white, are equal and of the same family.

Today our people have a crisis, and this crisis began when the white man came to this continent. The problem is this: It has been the mandate of our people to look after the welfare of the land and its life. Central to this responsibility is a recognition and respect for the equality of all of the elements of life on this land. Recognition and respect for the equality of all elements of life is necessary because it brings us into perspective as human beings. If all life is considered equal, then we are no more or no less than anything else. Therefore, all life must be respected. Whether it is a tree, a deer, a fish, or a bird, it must be respected because it is equal. We believe it is equal because we are spiritual people. If a tree is standing there, then the Creator must have put it there, and if the Creator has put it there, then you must respect it. If a person is sitting there, obviously the Creator has made this person; therefore, you must respect the person. If we are to put this belief into practice, then we must protect life and all its manifestations.

We human beings, however, have been given an added responsibility. We have been given an intellect – that is, the ability to decide for ourselves whether we will do a thing this way or that way. The human being has been given the gift to make choices, and he has been given guidelines, or what we call original instructions. This does not represent an advantage for the human being but rather a responsibility. All the four colours of mankind received those original instructions, but somewhere in time, in many places, they have been lost. It is a credit to us native people that we have retained those instructions. Many non-Indians have tried to destroy the original instructions because they view them as detrimental to progress.

It is important for us Indians to understand that we are being subjected to a process that has as its primary purpose the removal of our identity as native people. I was in Havana two years ago and I asked, 'Are there any Indians here?' They said, 'Oh no, there are only Cubans.' I was in Canada and I said, 'Where are the Indians?' They said, 'We have only Canadians here.' In the United States they want us all to be American citizens. You see, there is a process involved here, to remove our native identity. The reason that they want to remove our native identity is that as long as we native people, who are indigenous to the land, exist, we have claim to the land. That claim in international legal terms is called 'aboriginal title.' That claim to the land has always been the issue, and it will remain the issue as long as we exist.

Is it worth the effort to keep our unique identity, to keep our ways, to keep our land? This is the fundamental question that we must ask ourselves today. Is it worth the effort? The wars between the nations, English, French, and native, are still going on. We can observe this in the conflict over bilingualism in Canada. Empires are built on language. When we speak their languages, we come under their empire. If you think that language is not important, then why are all instructions in Canada printed in French and in English? Because if the instructions were written only in English, then the French would be defeated. If they were written only in French, then the English would be defeated. And if we native people give up our languages, then we are defeated.

One of the big problems in American and Canadian societies, and, in fact, in all Western societies, is the lack of understanding of time. They do not understand what is old and what is not. To judge what is old, you must have an appropriate measuring stick. If you are going to measure everything in terms of your own lifetime, which is the way Western societies tend to measure time today, then you are going to misjudge time. 'Old' in Western society is perhaps one hundred, three hundred, three thousand years. But that is not really very old. Indian people have a better understanding of time. They understand that an ant's time on this earth is very short and that the time of mountains and rivers is very long. Mankind falls somewhere in between. But our life-span certainly is not an adequate measuring stick of time.

Unfortunately, most of the decisions that are being made today by governments in Western societies have as their point of reference the life-span of man or, worse still, the term of office of the decision-makers. The result is some very short-sighted policies. A society in which decisions are made with reference to four-year election terms will encounter many problems. If not our generation then certainly the next is going to suffer from the short-sighted decisions that are made under such a system of government.

Imagine a circle divided into four parts by directional arrows. This is a universal symbol that all indigenous peoples recognize and understand immediately. The centre of that circle is the family, and at the heart of it is the woman. Just as Mother Earth is the core of life, so the woman as mother is the core of her family. The family sits in a circle, and that circle is called a clan. The clans in turn also sit in a circle, and that circle is called a nation. Then these nations sit in a circle, and that is called the world. Finally, there is the universe, which is the largest of the circles. The symbolism is meaningful, and it is important. It belongs not only to indigenous people but to all people. Eventually, I think, all peoples will begin to realize the importance of that particular symbol, the circle and the four quarters.

We native people understand that all living things are one large extended family and that we therefore should be working together in all the four corners of the world. We say there exists a common interest that should determine the future of the world. The common interest should be, as it is stated by my people, the welfare of the seventh generation to come. Every decision should be made in reference to how that decision will affect the seventh generation in the future.

The destructive effects of short-term thinking can already be seen in the damage that has been inflicted on our environment. There is much damage being done right now, and people are going to suffer for it later on. This is especially the case with our water resources. Water is the very basis of life. If you don't eat for fifteen or twenty days, you will probably survive, depending on how tough you are. But how many days can you go without water? Try it sometime. Just don't drink any water for a day or two and see what your body tells you. Water is the source of life. When you pollute the water, when you pollute the wells and springs, it is going to take hundreds of years to clean them up. What have you done to future generations? And for what purpose? You are taking a profit now at the expense of your grandchildren. Native people are concerned about the survival of all grandchildren everywhere.

We have two major forces in this world. One is communism and the other is capitalism. At present there is a huge philosophical battle going on between these two forces, an economic battle, really, because every-thing comes down to economics. Indigenous people are caught right in the middle of this battle. What are we going to do? We see this dilemma of indigenous people manifested clearly in El Salvador. The American and Canadian people fear the Russians going into El Salvador. Well, if you talked with the indigenous people of El Salvador you would discover that they wouldn't know a Russian if they bumped into one, but they know what oppression is. They also know what military might is, and the meaning of death. They do not see their condition of poverty and oppression as a philosophical issue.

One of the statements made in the United States Congress is that American Indians live in a communistic style because they hold land in common. The capitalistic principle is, simply stated, private property and all that accrues to private property. We native people did not have the concept of private property in our lexicon, and the principle of private property was pretty much in conflict with our value system. For example, you wouldn't see 'No Hunting,' 'No Fishing,' or 'No Trespassing' signs in our territories. To a native person such signs would have been equivalent to saying 'No Breathing' because the air is somebody's private property. If you said to the people, 'The Ontario government owns all the air in Ontario, and if you want some, you are going to have to go and see the Bureau of Air,' we would all laugh. Well, it made the Indians laugh too when the Europeans said, 'We are going to own the land.' How could anyone *own* the land? Well, today if you take a flight across the country, you will see all the little squares down below. You know, every inch of that land is 'owned' by someone.

Land is the central issue. That is what the American and Canadian governments want – our land and everything that lies under it. When the European colonizers began arriving on our shores in great numbers, we came to international agreements with them, treaties about land ownership. You should understand that treaties have nothing to do with law. They are political agreements. This is the way international politics is conducted. For example, in order for Israel and Egypt to sit down, discuss, and come to some kind of resolution of their problems, they had to do it without the restrictions of either government's law. They did it as separate sovereign political entities. It had nothing to do with law. Once the agreement is made, then it is incumbent upon each nation to have some kind of vehicle by which these agreements can be carried out. That is where law comes in, to carry out the agreement.

We live in a capitalistic state. The motivating force behind capitalism is greed. Capitalists have taken greed – that is, the idea of taking for yourself – and have used greed as a motor force for capitalism. Capitalists have built a whole system around greed. The main features of such a society that make it different from other societies are the profit motive and the process by which profit will accrue, and to whom it accrues. Mostly it accrues to major international corporations, which are often more powerful than any single country and which have more of an economic base than many of the countries in the world. They have interests all over the world, and they are not necessarily loyal to any nation. This is where our governments have a problem today. They have spawned these large corporate powers, and these corporate powers have the wealth by which they can buy the best talent. They can buy expertise, time, and anything they need. They can buy political officials, and they do. Often they have enough power to become the determining factor in what government policy will be.

Communism, on the other hand, represents state control. There is no private property. Communism is a word that has as many meanings as there are countries that espouse it. Chinese communism is not the same as Russian communism. And neither of these are identical to Cuban communism. But basically, communism is a form of state power. All the services, such as education, health, welfare, transportation, all of that is supposedly free. Goods such as clothes and food are often rationed, but they are supposed to be distributed evenly. This is the primary ideology of communism, that there is no individual wealth and that all people share equally. Having observed communism at close hand, I saw that there was a great deal of bureaucracy involved. There were many lines of people waiting for hours to buy goods. For some goods they must wait for days, even months and years. On the other hand, the people looked healthy and well fed.

What do these two forces have in common? The first thing both have in common is industrial development. Both have a total commitment to industrial development and technology. Now, there is nothing wrong with technology, and I want to make it clear that when the Creator gave us our brains, he intended us to use these brains for the development, protection, and welfare of our people. There is nothing in the native Indian value system restricting us from using technology. Technology is a creation of the human intellect. Therefore, it is not bad in and of itself. But for what purpose is it to be used? Herein lies the problem. Is it to be used for the welfare of the people or for the welfare of the corporation? Our people have an old philosophical story about a silver and gold serpent that eventually grows so large that it devours everything, including the people. What does that mean? What is the silver and gold serpent? The industrial state also consumes people and resources.

Another similarity between capitalism and communism is the way they reach decisions. The capitalists use an executive committee. An executive committee is a small committee that has tremendous power, and its work is done mainly in secret. It has the power to close the door and exclude you from the process of decision-making. Although we don't know what goes on in all those important meetings they have, we do know that they are involved in a process of accruing wealth, private property. The communists, on the other hand, have their central committee. The central committee represents a centralization of power in the hands of a few people. Like the executive committee it also works in secret. Its goal is to expand and increase its control over the peoples and nations of the world.

What else do they have in common? Well, the communists disavow religion. They are antireligion. They don't want anything to do with it. They put all their faith in the state and in the ability of mankind to fend for itself. But what about the capitalists, who have wave upon wave of religious zealots? This continent was taken over on religious grounds. It was the Pope who laid down the mandates for the acquisition of territory. But is that religion? Well, we native people say that it may be religion but it is not spiritual, and there is a difference. We see capitalism as spiritually bankrupt. Even though capitalists cherish their religions and even though they go to church, these churches or organized religions are in fact centres of power. They are businesses. They have large landholdings. They are extremely powerful. They have huge amounts of money in their coffers. Has this anything to do with spirituality? We say it has to do with political power. It has to do with ideological positions and with imposing conceptions of the 'right way' on everyone else. This is what the 'moral majority' is attempting to do. (The very term 'moral majority,' like 'defensive bombing,' is a contradiction.) We say that capitalism and communism are both spiritually bankrupt.

Where does that leave us, the indigenous people? They call us Indian, but Indian means indigenous. It means we are the protectors of the land and all life in it. We are the spiritual centre and always have been. That is what we have to offer this warring world at this time in history. This is our political position, and the warring factions are threatening to exterminate us for it. But we must not sell out to them. There is an old Indian story about this fat dog who, while running about in the woods, runs into his old friend the wolf. The wolf, who hasn't had much to eat, is skinny, scruffy, and covered with burdocks. The fat dog shares some of his food with the wolf and, because he feels sorry for the wolf, invites the wolf to come and live with him. As they walk towards the town, the wolf looks at the fat dog and sees a worn spot around his neck, and asks what caused it. The dog tells him that sometimes he has to wear a collar. The wolf asks him why. The dog explains that he has to do certain things like be a watch-dog and wear this collar to get fed. The wolf stops in his tracks and says, 'I prefer to go back into the woods.' The wolf is Indian. The buffalo is Indian. The bear is Indian. The eagle is Indian. They are all members of our clans.

We Indians are in the spiritual centre of the world. We must hold on to what we have because we have 'the natural law.' The one thing you want to understand about nature and its laws is that there is no place for mercy, no compromising. It is absolute. If you don't wear enough clothes when you go hunting, you will freeze to death. The natural law prevails, regardless of what any international tribunal may decide. The natural law, in its most basic form, is simply that if you do not eat food, you will die; if you do not drink water, you will die. So will a dog, a deer, and anything that lives. We are all bound by this law. There is no way that you can violate this law and get away with it. It is basic, it is simple, and it is eternal. That is why it is important to understand that when a government develops laws to rule the people, it must develop those laws in accordance with the natural law; otherwise, the laws will fail. But the two great political powers on this earth are acting, in many cases, in direct conflict with the natural law. It is an amazingly egocentric and short-sighted attitude.

If Indian government is to mean anything, the first thing we must do is to determine who we are. We alone must make that political decision. We cannot go and ask someone, 'Who am I? Please give me an identity.' We must define our own identity. My people say, 'We are the Ho-dé-no-sau-nee. We are a nation and always have been a nation.' For the Indian nations there is no United States and Canada. We have never recognized the border. The border is a relatively new idea introduced by the colonizers. We have Six Nations people in both countries, and we say that the border is above our head. We walk back and forth below it. That line does not involve us.

Our Ho-dé-no-sau-nee nation has its own passport, and we did not ask anybody if we could make this passport. My Ho-dé-no-sau-nee passport has a Canadian and an American stamp on it. What does that mean? It means that we can travel wherever we want. Other nations must accommodate us. We have travelled all over Europe and to many other nations on our passport. That is a political statement, a definition of oneself and one's people. I bring this to your attention to illustrate that there are actions that you can take. But I must caution you that there is a great deal of responsibility associated with such an action. When you have people travelling abroad, you are responsible for their welfare, because as a nation you are responsible for your citizens.

Finally, let me make one more point. When our young people speak and make demands from their Indian governments, the Indian leaders have the responsibility to listen to these young people because it is their lives and their future that are at stake.

TOM PORTER

Traditions of the Constitution of the Six Nations

There have been many problems in Indian country in the last few years, especially in Mohawk country. The land of the Six Nations or Iroquois people, where I come from, is located in the St Lawrence Valley. When I say Iroquois, let me make a clarification. Iroquois means Mohawk nation, Oneida nation, Onandaga nation, Cayuga nation, Seneca nation, and, later on, when the pioneers chased the Tuscaroras out of North Carolina, they came north and became the sixth nation. All of these nations together constitute Iroquois.

The neighbour that borders us to the south is the state of New York. The neighbour to the north-east is the province of Quebec, and the neighbour to the north-west is Ontario. The Mohawks are surrounded. Our community is called Akwesasne, but the French and English people call it St Regis. Canada claims that half of it is located in Canada. The United States claims that the other half is located in the United States. If you ask the Mohawks, they will say it is in neither of those countries. This is the way it has been told to us by our elders, and that is the way we believe it to be.

I am not an official representative of the Mohawk government but a friend who tries to do the best I can to make things good for the Mohawks with whatever knowledge I have gathered since I was born. The foundation of my life, my values, and my dignity I owe to my late grandma. This summer, when the lilacs bloom, will be the third year of her passing. She did not speak English, but she was the foundation of what I am. She was the most wonderful woman in the entire world. When I was young, she taught me the values of what is right and what is good. When I grew up in the Onandaga country, Seneca country, Cayuga country, Oneida country, and in Mohawk country, all those old chiefs, who have now gone to the spirit world, also were an inspiration to me in discerning what is right and what is good. They were the ones who told us youngsters to grow straight and grow good. They were the ones who told us to have dignity. If it were not for the teachings of grandma and grandpa and those old leaders who never went to school, not even kindergarten, who were called 'illiterates' by Canadian and American experts, I would not have learned what is right and what is good. So I want to acknowledge them as the basis of my thoughts.

In the last decade or so Indian people across the countries of Canada and the United States have been experiencing what might be called a revitalization. We have awakened just in time to rediscover something that might otherwise have passed from our memory and from our reality forever. I am referring to our great heritage, our culture, and our values. Fortunately, we woke up in time. But when you wake up, the day just begins, so we still have a long way ahead of us and a lot of work to do now that we have awakened. In this reawakening we hear different communities talking about 'Indian government.' I never thought about it very much before because in the community where I was raised my world was small and I did not have much understanding of other things in the world. I had never considered that there are many ways to look at Indian government.

Whenever one mentions Indian government to me or to the Iroquois people, the number-one thing that we think about, right off the bat, is that the person is talking about the government that the Creator gave to the Indian people, before Christopher Columbus made his mistake and came here. So that is what we think about right away when you say 'Indian government.' It is not in our mind whatsoever that Indian government has anything to do with parliamentary procedure. It is not in our mind whatsoever that Indian government has anything to do with the Indian Act. It is not in our mind whatsoever that Indian government has anything to do with the Department of Indian Affairs. To us those ideas are all as if they came from the farthest planet in the universe. This is how I am going to approach the subject.

The Iroquois people or the Ho-dé-no-sau-nee people were given a Constitution more than one thousand years ago by a Messiah that the Creator sent to North America to stop war and the evilness and sadness that come about when there is war and killing. The Messiah sought to introduce Indian government and Indian law to stop war and killing. This Messiah did miraculous things; he was certainly the equivalent of any other great prophet of the world. This Messiah, the Peacemaker, introduced a law to ban Indian warfare, and he gave us a formula for a constitutional government. This was probably the first constitutional government in the world and certainly one of the longest lasting. Our people still follow that law, that Constitution, and that formula for peace. That is the Indian government I wish to talk about.

One can approach an understanding of Mohawk government by thinking of a circle. The same approach can be used to understand the government of the Oneidas, Onandagas, Cayugas, Senecas, and so forth. That circle is the Mohawk nation. Think of the circle as a pie, and the pie is divided into nine sections. Before I go on to explain the pie, first let me tell you that the Mohawk nation is a matriarchal society. In Canadian society you follow your father's line. If his name was Johnson, then your name will be Johnson. But in Iroquois country we follow the mother's line and the clan she comes from. All her children and grandchildren are identified with her clan. Now, back to the pie. Each of the nine pieces of the pie represents one clan. Let us take the Bear clan, because it is the clan I come from. If you understand the way the Bear clan works, you will also understand the other eight clans, like the Wolf and Turtle and so on. The Bear clan is made up of men, women, children, nieces, nephews, and so forth. There may be about one thousand persons in any one clan. This clan is divided into two parts. One part consists of women, the other part of men. There are also two councils: a women's council and a men's council.

According to our Constitution, we have a chief. But the chief is not like a chief executive or commander-in-chief, as non-Indians seem to think of a chief. He does not have power or high status, like a king or a dictator. This is not the way it is with our leaders. Our term for leader comes from a root word that means 'nice' or 'good,' and that is what we call our leaders. This is a big difference from the English word 'chief.' For purposes of simplification, however, I will call our leader a chief.

Nine male chiefs, each representing one clan, make up the Mohawk nation's council. For every man chief, there is a woman chief, whom we call a clan mother. The woman chief is in charge of selecting the man chief for her clan. This is her duty, according to the thousand-year-old mandate from the Creator. Once he is selected, providing he is good and does things according to his people's best welfare, the chief is a leader for the rest of his life. But if he makes a serious mistake, then the clan mother has the authority to remove him from that office through a special process. That process, in Westernized terms, is an impeachment process. In our nation we have had that process for over one thousand years, and relatively recently it was adopted by the United States.

As I said before, the Mohawk council is made up of the nine chiefs of the Mohawk nation. All of their decisions have to be by consensus. There is no majority rule. Every one of them has to agree, or the law is not law. Let us say that these nine men are sitting in council and suddenly one chief takes a notion to be contrary. For no good reason other than his own selfishness, he causes the council not to have a consensus. When this happens, the clan mother who selected him will observe him. If she feels that he is being contrary out of selfishness, she can call him out and talk to him. There are special words that she will use. She will say, 'You know our clan has selected you because we trusted you and you were kind all of your life as you were growing up. We watched you grow from a baby, and you were always good. But now you are acting strangely, and it is not in the interest of our family or our nation. We need you and we want you.' She continues with special words to make the chief feel good. Then she will say, 'Now, my son, go back and sit in the council and do the proper thing for which we have selected you.' He will go back to the council, and the woman watches. If he does not stop being contrary, then the clan mother will get some of the faith-keepers and they will go talk to him and remind him again of his duty. If he doesn't listen, well, then he is a bad apple right there. That is not good. That is not what a chief is supposed to be like. So if he does that two times, the third time there is no warning. The clan mother will tell one of the men (a big one) to go over and remove the horn off his head, which is the symbol of his leadership. That is what we call impeachment – dehorned. That is the greatest shame that can ever happen to a man. When that happens to a chief, our leaders say that he has become 'a walking dead.'

My grandfather told me that, in times past, if a man became dehorned and brought shame to his family and his people, they would scar him on the left side of the face or clip the ear on the left side in a certain manner. He would then be told, 'Go look over this world because, the way you are, you will never find peace among us. So go and search this world, and maybe you can find some other people who think like you and that is where you will find peace.' My grandma's uncle said that a man who had that scar on his face would go towards the west, and, as he walked into the bush, even the deer and the beavers, who knew the law, would see that scar and turn the other way. If he came to Blackfoot country, the Blackfoot knew the law, and they too would have nothing to do with him. That is why it was said, 'His feet are hanging on the edge of the world.' This punishment is the greatest shame we can experience. I knew one man whom it happened to, and that man ran away from his people in shame. He was a walking dead. He was fifty-one years old, and he died from a broken heart. He died over one thousand miles from his people. So our Indian government is nothing to mess with. It is serious business. It is meant for peace. It is meant for the unity of the people, and to raise the people in good health.

If a chief dies in the Mohawk nation, the Onandagas, Senecas, and Mohawks go into mourning. There are tears in our eyes. Our hearts are saddened, and our ears are deafened by the tragedy. We can't think properly, and this is why, before we set about selecting another leader, 'the younger brothers' – that is, the Oneidas, the Cayugas, and the Tuscaroras – have to travel from their country to my country to offer condolences and to take away our sorrow. Their words are beautiful. They say, 'We took a deer skin from the sky and we wipe the tears from your eye, you, our older brother. We took the eagle's feather from the sky and we brush away the dust of death from your ears, so that you may hear again the birds singing and your children laughing. We give you this good medicine to take the knots and the yellow things from your stomach because of death.' This is the way and teaching of our great-grandfathers. Our government and our Constitution is set up that way. So the Oneidas, Cayugas, and Tuscaroras must come and console us, and when they have consoled us, we raise another leader for the Mohawks. We do the same thing for them if one of their leaders dies; we, the Mohawks, Onandagas, and Senecas go to be with them, our younger brothers.

When a leader dies, his position becomes empty, and the selection of a new leader, as I said, is the duty of the clan mother. How do we make a new leader? Before I describe that, let me explain why the women are the ones who select the men to be the leaders. This is because, in our traditional beliefs, the earth is our mother. She is the one who supports all life. Like the mother earth, the human mother is the one who carries the child, and when the child is born, the mother feeds and cares for the child. If the child makes just a tiny noise in the night, the mother jumps right up to care for it. She can hear the slightest noise that the child makes. So, you see, the Creator made the woman more sensitive than the man in certain respects. That is a natural fact. Then when that little boy or girl grows a little bigger and starts to run around and gets burdocks in his hair or her hair, usually it is the mother who takes the burdocks out and strings the hair up.

My grandma and the old leaders at home used to say, 'It is the mother who knows her children better than anybody else does.' So if you want to get a reference on someone, you go and find that person's mother and ask her what the person is like, because she knows. If that child, as he was growing up, was stingy, selfish, or if that child was mean or moody, the mother will know that. So when it comes time to make leaders, they ask the woman, 'Who amongst all your sons or nephews is of good quality? Who amongst all of your relatives has the natural goodness to be a chief?' The mother will be the one to know, and that is why in our nation the woman was chosen for this duty.

When choosing a new leader, it is not unusual for all the women of the clan to organize a big meeting. During this meeting they will review all their sons in that clan and ask questions such as, 'When this person was crawling around, was he a good baby? When that baby was running around, was he kind? Did he have a tendency to fight with his brother, cousin, or his own family?' The women research that person's background, right from a baby to adulthood. All the candidates are reviewed in this manner. The women do not reveal whom they are thinking of putting up as candidates. So there is no chance for a man to go around campaigning, to go around saying, 'Vote for me, I am going to do this for you or I am going to do that for you' – and then when he gets to be leader he doesn't do anything for you. That, you know, is the Canadian and American way. Under the Indian way, he does not know that he is a candidate, and so he does not do that. There are checks and balances existing all through the Indian way of government. You see, the Creator did it right.

Once the candidate has been elected, the clan mother (and all those women who helped her out) will give him over to the men, who also call a meeting for approval and confirmation of the women's choice. Why do they ask the men to check him out? Because, long ago, the men used to go hunting, about a dozen of them in each group, for two to three weeks in the Algonquin country to the north or to Mohican country in the south. When that hunter goes away, the women don't know how he behaves. Maybe when he goes up to Algonquin country he says he's not married and messes around with Algonquin girls. That is why the women have to get the candidate confirmed by the men, because they are the ones who go with him when he goes away. Today the situation is still the same. Iroquois men still go in groups of six to twelve to Los Angeles, San Diego, or Chicago. They are still foraging for a living, but it's iron-work this time, making bridges and tall buildings. So our system has checks and balances in it all the way through.

When a chief is chosen, he is told: 'Your skin has to be seven layers thick, because people will be ungrateful and they will throw sharp words at your heart when you are tired. You must not let the sharp words penetrate your heart. That is why your skin has to be seven layers thick.' A candidate for leadership must be married, and he has to have children. That is the Creator's first natural arrangement, for a woman and a man to come together to make a family to continue the nation's growth. The nation is always considered to be the chief's first wife, and his married wife will always be the second wife. That means the business of the nation comes before all else. A candidate for leadership is also judged on the basis of whether he attended all of the nation's ceremonies and spiritual rituals. Did he on his own initiative attend the harvest ceremonies? Did he always want to go, and did he always dance in the ceremonies? He has to know those ceremonies because the knowledge of the spiritual values of his nation is the chief's first mandate from the Creator. When he has passed all the tests and he has been approved by the women and the men, the Oneidas and Cayugas come to confirm him. He has to pass their inspection as well. Then we get a new leader.

A chief cannot get angry with his people. He cannot call anyone down. He must speak with kind words at all times. If you go to where the chiefs live in the tradition of the Mohawks, you will notice something peculiar. Their houses are usually the most humble and the smallest, because they are always giving to the people of their nation. How much you have given since you were a baby is one of the criteria that the women take into consideration when they select a leader. What counts is how much you gave to others, not how outstanding you were at this or that. Every leader in the Mohawk nation, Oneida nation, Onandaga nation, Cayuga nation, and Seneca nation is chosen in this manner.

Our chiefs cannot go to war; they would forfeit their claims to be peace chiefs. If they do go to war, they must give their leadership back to the clan mother while the war goes on. If they kill someone in that war, they will never get their horn or leadership back because they are peace chiefs. These are just some of the things that I was told by my old people. These are some of the characteristics of a great natural human government that was given to us by the Messiah and the Creator of our people.

So when you say 'Indian government' to the Iroquois, Mohawks, Oneidas, Onandagas, Cayugas, or Senecas, we think about the Creator's law, not parliamentary procedure. We don't associate it with the prime minister or the president. There is no room in Indian government for people who seek power, fame, and notoriety. Indian government seeks humble men, as humble as you can find in the world, because they must give and give and cry and cry for their people. When the gardens are not good and there is a scarcity of food, the leaders will be the last ones to eat. First come the children, then the old ones, then the rest of the people, and if there is anything left over, then the chief will eat. Traditional Indian government is foolproof because it is based on integrity, justice, and real democracy.

We are talking about the nationhood that God gave us, nothing else, because we are the indigenous natural people. We in the East, the Iroquois, are having nothing to do with Canada's Constitution or the American Constitution, because the Creator gave us our own Constitution over one thousand years ago. When Indian leaders seek Indian government, they take the guidance of the Creator. They talk with humbleness because they talk for their children, for their wives, nieces, and nephews, and for their grandmothers, who, like mine, may have passed away. They talk for the good of all their people, past, present, and future generations. They do not seek fame or fortune because that is what makes corruption, and we don't need that. We are already in a bad enough way. The day is new, and we have a lot of work to do in this day.

2 Ethnonationalist Ideas

POLITICAL DEVELOPMENTS since World War II illustrate that ethnic national consciousness as a political force is in the ascendancy. Armed with the doctrine of self-determination, a growing number of ethnic minorities are challenging the nation-states within which they exist. As the contributions in this section illustrate, the quest for greater autonomy by Canada's native Indian peoples is part of a wider movement encompassing a number of countries and indigenous groups. In many respects, Indian peoples in Canada confront the same impediments as other indigenous peoples in their struggle for decolonization.

Rudolph Ryser, in his discussion of indigenous movements in North and South America, argues that the patterns of colonial oppression are everywhere fundamentally the same. All indigenous peoples have been subject to 'the great lie' that European ideas and values are superior. The great lie has functioned as a subterfuge for the elimination of the indigenous peoples as distinct nations and for exploitation of their lands and resources.

In another selection, Marie Marule advances the same thesis. She asserts that Canada's native Indians suffer from a sense of inferiority about their traditional ways of life and institutions. This is reflected in the submissive and subordinate manner in which native Indians deal with the federal government and with non-Indians. What is now needed, she argues, is unilateral action by Indians to implement forms of Indian government and political institutions that are based on revitalized traditional beliefs.

Finally, Kirke Kickingbird discusses the idea of sovereignty held by American Indians, a concept that is finding increasing expression in the political stance of Canada's native peoples. Kickingbird also explores the barriers that exist to the implementation of self-government by American Indian tribes.

RUDOLPH C. RYSER

Nation-States, Indigenous Nations, and the Great Lie

In this paper I will analyse the relationship of selected indigenous nations in various parts of the world to the governments of the countries in which they are found. I have selected for analysis the United States, Canada, Chile, and Nicaragua. These countries have been selected for three reasons. One, the policies of these nation-states towards indigenous nations have all been drawn from the American governmental experience. Two, these indigenous populations share common political, economic, and social aspirations. Three, they all illustrate relationships that have resulted from what I call 'the great lie.'

In my opinion, nowhere does a *model of relations* exist between indigenous populations and nation-states that is acceptable to indigenous peoples. There are, however, hundreds of examples of nation-state and indigenous-nation relations where the dominant political and economic interests practise deception aimed at the elimination of indigenous nations. It is my intent to answer three questions in this paper: What is the great lie? How has the great lie been used by nation-states to control and then eliminate indigenous nations? Finally, what are the alternatives available to indigenous nations if they are to avoid ultimate and final destruction by nation-states?

Indian nations are made up of peoples who are the descendants of the original landlords of territories occupied for thousands of years. These Indian nations are the successor nations to great civilizations that dominated the world for thousands of years. By contrast, the nation-states within which these indigenous people are found today are political organizations that have come into existence only in the last two-hundred-year period. By various means they have sought to expand

their influence throughout the indigenous nations, surrounding indigenous peoples and establishing colonial regimes designed to confiscate
indigenous lands and natural resources while suppressing and extermi-
nating the political identity of whole indigenous nations. The contemporary reality is that indigenous nations do continue to exist, though
greatly weakened, while the nation-states have grown larger, more
powerful, and more threatening to the indigenous nations.

The nation-states of Canada, the United States, Nicaragua, and Chile
have come to dominate and repress indigenous nations principally by
means of what I call 'the great lie.' Though each of the nation-states
began its existence as a politically and economically weak group of
people with only a small foothold on the territory, the people of these
fledgling nations used their weakness to gain help and support from the
more powerful indigenous nations. Indigenous nations permitted the
small and helpless nations to organize governments and even to increase
their populations by allowing increased entry of political and economic
refugees from other nations in Europe. During this process the great lie
began to have importance as a political and economic tool for the new
nations occupying indigenous territories.

As a means to gain greater concessions and aid from indigenous
nations, the new European nations began the selective process of con-
vincing indigenous peoples that it is the destiny of European nations to
govern, control, and exploit the indigenous peoples, lands, and resources.
The European nations, so they argued, had the right to govern the world
because they were superior beings. Indigenous peoples, on the other
hand, were primitive, savage, and incompetent. Indigenous peoples
should be treated as non-humans. The theory was that if enough indigenous people could be convinced of their own incompetence and that
their own political, economic, and cultural systems were evil, then they
would reject their own indigenous nations. Once indigenous people
rejected their own values and systems, they could then be drawn into the
European nation and be effectively controlled.

The new European nations have worked diligently to wipe out indigenous history and intellectual thought and replace these with European
history and intellectual thought. The great lie is simply this: *If indigenous
peoples will only reject their own history, intellectual development, language,
and culture and replace these things with European values and ideals, then
indigenous people will survive.* It is from this twisted thinking that Euro-

pean nations have convinced millions of indigenous people all over the world to surrender their freedom and accept subjugation as a way of life.

Nowhere in the world has the great lie had a greater success than in the United States. After many years of writing treaties and forcing indigenous nations to agree to their contents, the United States government would systematically violate those same agreements. To excuse these violations, the United States would tell the indigenous nations that, since they were incapable of understanding the agreements in the first place, the United States would use its *own* system of justice to find a remedy for treaty conflicts – not international law or the laws of indigenous nations. Since 1831 the United States has been adjudicating disputes between itself and indigenous nations. History has demonstrated that the more dependent indigenous nations become upon American legal and political institutions, the more they experience erosion of their own governmental powers, territorial and natural-resource rights, and cultural development.

The United States did not stop at simply asserting its superiority over indigenous nations through its legal system. After 1871, when the United States unilaterally declared its intention to cease treaty-making with indigenous nations, it imposed a new concept on its relations with indigenous peoples. It asserted that the Congress of the United States would exert *plenary power* over all matters involving indigenous nations. In more direct terms, the American government declared that it would exercise absolute and unlimited political power over the internal and external affairs of indigenous nations. The United States installed a legislative dictatorship over the affairs of indigenous peoples within the newly established United States boundaries. In fact, the United States government declared indigenous governments illegal and asserted that such governments would be forcibly suppressed. Indian nations would be cut off from the world family of nations.

In 1934 the U.S. Congress enacted a law called the Indian Reorganization Act, designed effectively to replace any vestige of the original indigenous governments with governments to be designed and implemented by the United States itself. These governments would be recognized by Congress as the legitimate governments over indigenous territories. The constitutions for the American-made indigenous governments placed all of the political authority of government under the control of an appointed bureaucrat, the secretary of the Interior, and the legislative power in the

U.S. Congress. These tribal governments were granted limited powers to enact laws, but they were granted substantial powers to regulate and control tribal people on behalf of the United States. In a very real way, these tribal governments became direct extensions of the United States government, operating under U.S. laws and policies. These tribal governments in effect became colonial governments. The rules under which these colonial tribal governments operated ensured U.S. access to and control over indigenous peoples, lands, and natural resources.

Indigenous political leaders did not at first agree to the U.S.-sponsored colonial-government system. Indeed, many indigenous political leaders actively opposed U.S. intervention in indigenous political and legal affairs. Many of these leaders were able to convince their own peoples not to accept the U.S.-designed tribal-government system. Yet other political leaders within indigenous nations accepted money, guarantees of political power, and other gifts from the United States in exchange for their support of the colonial tribal-government system. While many indigenous nations retained their own government systems, a greater number did accept U.S. government authority. Now, forty-seven years later, many indigenous political leaders are questioning the wisdom of accepting U.S.-sponsored Indian governments. Indeed, many indigenous nations have discovered that under this system the rights and interests of indigenous peoples have been overwhelmingly subordinated to the interests of the United States. Tribal economies, political structures, and cultural systems have been eroded or destroyed.

Indigenous peoples in the United States have become refugees in their own land. They have become hostages to the American legal and political system. Indigenous law and political development is being vigorously suppressed. The timber, oil, coal, uranium, water, and land belonging to the indigenous nations are being used by the United States to benefit that country's goals and aspirations, while the invented tribal-government system is being used against indigenous peoples to deny them the sole use of their own property.

An American-invented educational system is being forced on indigenous populations to ensure that succeeding generations of indigenous people will have completely forgotten the existence of indigenous nations. Indigenous children are being taught that George Washington was the founding father of their nation. They are being told that their nation is the United States and that the American political system was created to give freedom to the oppressed. They are being told that America is a beacon of freedom for all peoples. What they are not being told, however, is that the United States has sought to destroy their homeland, their history, their language, and their culture, as well as their freedom.

Deception through the great lie has permitted the United States, once a weak and defenseless nation, to become the dominant political and economic force throughout the Western Hemisphere. With their economies decimated, their governments in shambles, and their peoples in poverty, the indigenous nations now look to the United States government for help and for sustenance. The United States and its corporations say only, 'Give us your land, your minerals, your petroleum, and your water, and we will give you your freedom.' This may seem a harsh indictment of the United States, but let me remind you that if you ask about the present condition of indigenous peoples in the United States and try to explain how that condition came to be, you must conclude that it resulted from the actions of traitors among indigenous peoples, or from the actions of deceitful Europeans, or from the actions of both. I subscribe to the view that indigenous nations have been deceived by the Europeans with the help of indigenous traitors who gave their loyalty to the United States and turned against the indigenous nations.

In many ways, the situation in Canada resembles the stage of political development in the United States during the latter nineteenth century and the early twentieth century. Both the nation of Canada and the nation of the United States were born of the same mother. The United States gained release from its mother over two hundred years ago. Canada has just recently severed the umbilical cord, called the British North America Act, by which it was tied to its mother. Like the United States, Canada wants to become a full-grown power able to act on its own without following the rules set down by the mother. Unlike the United States, Canada had to wait a long time before asking the royal mother if it could leave home and grow up. Everything Canada knows about conducting relations with indigenous nations it learned either from its mother or from its bigger brother, the United States. Just as the United States made agreements and broke them with indigenous nations, so has Canada. Just as the United States created a legislative dictatorship over indigenous nations, so has Canada.

Now Canada is at a crossroad. Belatedly separated from the mother, it views the indigenous nations as an obstacle. Canada cannot claim to be an independent country unless it exercises full control over the territory within its boundaries – over, that is, all of the people, all of their land, and all of the natural resources. The indigenous nations in Canada have learned from the mistakes of their brothers to the south and they are not prepared to give Canada control over their people, lands, and natural resources. To remedy this problem, the Canadian government is now seeking to follow the example of its brother in the south by promoting the parliamentary enactment of an Indian-government act. This act is, for all practical purposes, a direct copy of the U.S. Indian Reorganization Act. In fact, the Canadian government has consulted extensively with U.S. officials over the years to learn about the model policies and approaches that Americans used so successfully in subjugating their indigenous governments.

While Canada's administrative structure is somewhat different from that of the United States, it has worked to accomplish the same goals: the elimination of indigenous nations and the substitution of Canadian-European values for indigenous values. Assimilation of indigenous populations is the essential goal. Canada will be able to achieve its goal if Canadian officials can convince the indigenous people to believe the great lie. Paradoxically, the effort to assimilate indigenous peoples politically in Canada constitutes a tacit recognition by Canada that indigenous nations are wholly outside of the Canadian federal system.

Canadian officials know that 64 per cent of the territory known as Canada belongs to the indigenous nations and not to Canada. These are unceded territories. Canada cannot exercise full national dominion without controlling indigenous people, their lands, and their resources. So what they offer in exchange is recognition of Indian governments in the Constitution and in the laws. Just as the United States instituted Indian governments for its own ends, Canada is now proposing to institute such governments. Just as the United States sought to gain control over indigenous lands, resources, and people, Canada is now seeking such control. Canada has already worked to implement the great lie by telling indigenous peoples that the Canadian Constitution can and will protect indigenous nations and prevent further erosion of aboriginal rights. But Canadian officials offer indigenous peoples no control or political power in Canada's government. Indeed, indigenous leaders must understand unequivocally that Canada cannot permit their nations to continue to exist. For, as long as they exist, they will always be a threat to Canada's sovereignty and its political integrity as a nation-state.

The Canadian government has, time and time again, officially denied that the first nations of Canada, the indigenous nations, have original claim to the vast territories that are called Canada. They have denied that the first nations have a political identity separate from that federation called Canada. Canada insists on claiming political and economic rights within indigenous territories. To admit that such rights do not exist would create a situation in which it could be argued that Canada has only an administrative responsibility towards indigenous nations. So Canada's solution is to institute the great lie. 'We will help you, brothers. Come and join us and you can be yourselves.' But look at what happened in North America to the south. Many of the brothers are not a part of the family anymore. They are part of America.

In Nicaragua, we have a very similar situation. There are three indigenous tribes in Nicaragua, the Miskito, the Rama, and the Sumu. They occupy the eastern half of the country, where they make up the majority population. Under the Somoza regime, they were told that they must 'Be Nicaraguans, not Miskitos, not Ramas, not Sumus. You must be Nicaraguans, and if you are not to be Nicaraguans, then you will be dead.' Many of the people in those tribes revolted in 1978 against the Somoza regime, even though it was sustained in power by the United States and other Western powers. It was a revolution instituted by the indigenous people against an oppressive regime.

The Sandinista National Liberation Front (FSLN), Hispanic descendants, not indigenous people, who were the religious and labour leaders in Nicaragua, said, 'We will take the lead and we will save you from this madman Somoza.' So they took up the revolution against Somoza and they won in 1979, and everyone was proud, for now they were done with the oppression. The Miskitos, the Ramas, and the Sumus believed that they would now have an opportunity to have their own land and their own nations once again. But not long after the Sandinistas assumed leadership and control of Nicaragua, they went to the indigenous peoples and said, 'You are Nicaraguans. You are not Miskitos, you are not Ramas, you are not Sumus. If you are not Nicaraguans, you are dead.'

The Sandinistas offered to the Miskitos, Ramas, and Sumus a role in the new government. An organization called MISURASATA was formed to represent the more than 185,000 Indians. 'We will give you a government as a part of our government, and we will even permit you to have a representative in our government,' the Sandinistas said. They then went ahead and selected a person to represent the indigenous people in the parliament of the Sandinistas. So, where is the indigenous nation now? In February 1981, thirty-three leaders of MISURASATA were arrested. Security forces charged that the Indians were preparing a separatist movement. The Indians want to protect their territories from exploitation, and the Sandinistas want to extract minerals and metals from Indian soils. You see, the revolution to produce an indigenous nation must continue. The same controversy exists there as exists in Canada, as exists in the United States and everywhere where nation-states and indigenous nations collide. The central issue remains: Are the goals of nation-states the same as those of indigenous nations? All we can conclude by looking through history is no, they are not. Indigenous nations and nation-states can coexist, but if indigenous nations become part of a nation-state as subordinate peoples, then indigenous nations will disappear. The nation-states' urge to exploit indigenous peoples and their resources is overpowering.

In Chile, the situation is exactly the same. The new government of Pinochet advised the Mapuche people who had occupied the territory for thousands of years, 'You must move from that territory because there is copper and tin under your ground.' The Pinochet government urged the Mapuche to become full Chilean citizens and exercise their 'equal' rights. When they would not move, the Pinochet government enacted a law that says the government has the right to take the land. All they require is that one person, not necessarily a Mapuche but one person within the indigenous territory, say: 'Yes, you can have my land,' and then the government has the authority to take it all. And so they have. One hundred indigenous communities in the last year have been devastated. Their land has been opened up for mining copper, coal, zinc, nickel, and tin to advance the interests of Chile, to advance the interests of other peoples, but not to advance the interests of the Mapuche. Even their own land cannot benefit them now. The Mapuche have never played a role in the Chilean government – they are not a part of Chile.

The proclaimed superiority of the nation-state has, in each of our examples, been used to justify the dislocation and exploitation of indigenous nations. The 'laws of nations' have been subverted by domestic rationalizations to deny whole peoples their basic rights as human beings. The myth of superiority has been used to enrich colonial populations and impoverish indigenous peoples. The patterns of oppression are essentially the same. Indigenous nations in all of our examples have been surrounded by invading peoples leaving only tiny enclaves for indige-nous homelands. Each indigenous nation seeks to secure its homeland against further invasion. Each indigenous nation is denied its right to exercise its distinct political powers. The objective of each nation-state is the same: elimination of the indigenous population as a distinct nation and the exploitation of indigenous people, lands, and resources for the benefit of the nation-state.

What can be done? The answer is simple, and perhaps that is why it is so difficult. As our elders have said over and over again, through the centuries: 'Hold on to the nation of people. Defend the nation of people against all enemies. Assert your own government; you don't have to ask for a government. You have a government. If you have no government, you have no people; then there is nothing even to argue about.' All over the world today there are indigenous populations that carry out govern-mental activities as separate and distinct peoples, but too many feel they must ask the nation-state to give them the power to govern themselves. The only power that exists for any people, whether it is the United States or Canada, Shuswap or Blackfoot, Miskito or Mapuche, any nation, lies in the decision of the people to take the initiative, to conjure up the strength, to assert their nationhood to the rest of the world and say, 'We are here and we do not plan to disappear. Our power comes from within and from our access to the Great Spirit.' With those two things, the indigenous nation can survive. It cannot survive by asking someone else to allow it to exist.

The great lie must be rejected and replaced by a renewed dynamic among indigenous peoples. The indigenous nations are ancient in their origins – they are the seed of humankind. They must resume their role among the family of nations to reassert the balanced values that have ensured human survival on this planet.

MARIE SMALLFACE MARULE

Traditional Indian Government: Of the People, by the People, for the People

Our strength as Indians derives from our tribal identity. The Canadian government, very deliberately and systematically, is seeking to undermine our tribal identity by imposing policies on Indians that emphasize individualism and materialism. This policy of 'detribalization' subverts our consensual political system, our kinship system, our communal ownership system, and our collective economic system. This policy represents the biggest problem in our efforts to revitalize our Indian societies and governments.

In traditional Indian societies, whether band or clan, authority was a collective right that could be temporarily delegated to a leader, under restrictive conditions, to carry out essential activities. But the responsibility and authority always remained with the people.[1] In situations where the collectivity temporarily delegated authority to a leader, that person had to have the respect of the entire tribe, not merely the support of a majority of voters. Obedience to the leader derived from the respect that the people had for him. The coercive imposition by the Canadian government of an elected form of government on Indians is in direct conflict with traditional forms of government. The elective model is based on individual ownership of land and the delegation of authority from above, and it has created serious problems in our Indian communities. This is particularly true among the prairie tribes, where there has always been a strong tradition of decision-making by consensus rather than by individuals in authority.

I have had an opportunity to observe how the consensus approach to decision-making works in practice. In the mid-1970s when I worked for the executive council of the National Indian Brotherhood, they used this approach because they recognized a flaw in the system of majority rule. They saw that majority rule forces decisions on the minority, thereby creating divisions. The few times that the executive council attempted to use the majority-rule system of decision-making, it resulted in the abstention of those who didn't agree with it. They would not directly oppose it, but they did not pay any attention to it either. Thus, it was possible to work together only on those things where they all agreed. On matters of disagreement, each was left to take his own approach.

It is not known to what degree the Canadian government has been successful in its efforts to eliminate traditional Indian attitudes and values. It is assumed by many that very little remains of traditional Indian ideology and philosophy because the traditional Indian life-style is no longer in evidence; that is, we don't live in tepees anymore. This assumption holds that traditional values and beliefs changed when our life-styles changed. Implicit in this assumption, also, is the notion that Indian culture must remain static to remain Indian. But the history of our people is a history of successful adaptation to change while countering oppression and resisting imposition of undesired changes. A specific and important example of such resistance to imposed change can be observed in the Indians' refusal to submit to pressures by the Canadian government to adopt its system of individualized land allotment.

Why is the issue of Indian government taking centre stage at the present time? The answer is to be found in the policy goals of the Canadian government. They want to revise the Indian Act to accelerate the detribalization of Indians. Their ultimate goal is the termination of Indian status and the complete assimilation of our people into Canadian society. The first major attempt by the Canadian government to advance this objective was made in 1969. The 1969 White Paper on Indian policy sought to terminate Indian status and rights within a five-year period. It was unsuccessful. Now the Canadian government sees an opportunity to use the Constitution to achieve the same end. Embodied in the Constitution as it now stands is the falsehood that international political and legal principle gives to the Canadian government the right to terminate our special status as Indians. But if they truly have this right, why do they bother to pacify us by throwing a few words on aboriginal rights into the Canadian Charter of Rights and Freedoms? Why do they dangle the mirage of Indian government in front of us at this time? I say it is to divert our attention from their policy goals, which are in contravention of international political and legal principles.

When a delegation of the Union of British Columbia Indian Chiefs went to the United Nations to address the under-secretary-general of Political Affairs, Decolonization, and Trusteeships,[2] they said, 'Look here! You are ignoring us. You have addressed the colonial situations in Africa and Asia, but you have ignored the Western Hemisphere. Why is it that you are allowing colonial situations to exist in the Western Hemisphere?' Significantly, after the UBCIC brought this issue to the attention of the UN, the Canadian government suddenly became willing to negotiate changes to the Canadian Charter of Rights and Freedoms, adding protection for treaty and aboriginal rights along with traditional rights and freedoms. But this provision is not acceptable to the UBCIC because the charter contains no acceptable definitions of aboriginal and treaty rights. Furthermore, the provision governing Indian rights will be subject to the constitutional amending formula. This formula requires agreement by the provincial governments before any changes can be effected on Indian treaty and aboriginal rights.

It is no secret that the interests of the provincial governments are in direct conflict with Indian interests. This conflict of interest derives from Indian land claims. Currently, large parts of Canada are under tenancy by indigenous peoples. For example, 80 per cent of the population of northern Saskatchewan is native Indians; in northern Manitoba, it is 90 per cent. Now and historically these territories belonged to the indigenous people. Yet the consequence of the constitutional amending formula will be to leave Indians with whatever territories the provinces choose to surrender, which may be nothing. Some say that claiming these territories for Indians is a very idealistic and unrealistic position to take, a symbolic position. But that is not the position of the native people. The UBCIC rejected the proposed constitutional package, saying:

As long as we have no involvement in amendments that affect Indian people, then what we are offered is nothing. It is not better than what it was before. We are better off with S 91(24) of the BNA Act and the interpretation that administration of the trust now reverts back to Britain upon the independence of Canada.

To create division among Indians in their stand on the Constitution, the Canadian government decided to bait the constitutional trap. It leaked information that it was about to pass 'Indian-government' legislation that would empower Indian band councils to assume the authority currently exercised by the minister of Indian Affairs. By leaking news of this 'significant concession,' the Canadian government sought to induce some Indians to support the constitutional package. Even if this proposed 'concession' turns out to be genuine, however, it offers Canadian Indians no more than what the United States gave to its Indians in the Indian Reorganization Act of 1934. This is an act to institutionalize legal authority over Indians. For American Indians this act brought with it European concepts of authority and the associated structures, systems, and institutions. The Canadian Indian-government legislation is rumoured to have an 'opting-in' provision so that bands will not have to accept it if they do not want to. Ostensibly, bands will be allowed to opt into the Indian-government system when they are 'ready.' But there is an underlying threat that, if a band refuses to opt in when the government deems it should, its funds can be cut off.

The tactic of cutting off funds in order to coerce us to surrender our authority and responsibility is not new. The Canadian government used it during the last century by withholding rations in times of famine and disaster. Today social assistance is being manipulated in the same manner to subordinate and intimidate Indians. How can Indian people take political control of their communities when 80 per cent of them are dependent on the Canadian government for social assistance? We cannot declare political independence so long as we are dependent on Canadian government welfare.

In my travels, particularly in Central and South America, I have seen Indian communities that most of us would say are poor, and it is true that materially they are poor. But those people have a remarkable strength: they are independent economically. They feed themselves. They are not part of the national or international economic system. They are not consumers; they are producers: they produce all they need for themselves. This is in stark contrast to our Indians in North America. We are locked into the non-Indian economic system. We are hooked on consumerism.

Indian communities that have worked to get rid of their dependence on the Canadian government have not found it easy, but some have done it. The Neskainlith Indian people of the Shuswap nation have said,

We are going to do something about this dependency of ours. We are going to regain some degree of self-reliance. We are going to cut our dependency on money and on the Canadian government which controls every facet of our lives.

They are struggling to this end, and it is truly marvelous to see the progress they are making. They are showing that dependence is a matter of attitude.

There is a belief among some of our Indian people that by replacing the white bureaucrats in the Indian Affairs Department with brown people we will remedy all that is wrong with our situation. The experience of the United States Bureau of Indian Affairs (BIA) shows that this approach offers no solution to Indian problems. Sixty per cent of BIA employees are of native descent, and sixteen of the top twenty-five administrative positions are currently held by native people. Yet the BIA continues to function as an ineffective, oppressive agency because of its structure, its systems, and its processes. Currently some of our provincial organizations are acting on the assumption that by organizing themselves along the lines of the Indian Affairs Department they will be able to do more for their people than Indian Affairs now does. This too is a fallacy; furthermore, it is a fatal mistake for us to assume that solutions to our problems can be found in European-Western structures, systems, and processes.

Let us now turn to consider workable alternatives available to us. We talk about sovereignty and claim it for ourselves, but we have not yet begun to exploit the opportunities that are open to us to exercise it. British Columbia Indians have begun to take a leadership role in asserting their sovereignty. Why are British Columbia Indians more progressive than Alberta Indians in this regard? I have a personal theory about this: people living in poverty have less, individually, to lose and are more willing to risk what little they have to achieve their rights. In British Columbia, where there are smaller communities, a smaller land base, fewer resources, and less material wealth, Indians are willing to risk the consequences of confrontations with the Canadian government. In Alberta, where Indians have a larger land base, greater resources, and greater individual material wealth, they are acquiescing to the system that the Canadian government has imposed because they are afraid of losing what they have.

There exists in Alberta also a more entrenched Indian elite than one finds in British Columbia. This is because the benefits of economic development on Indian reserves tend to accrue to a privileged minority, and in Alberta there has been more economic development on Indian reserves. Emergence of an elite class in Alberta Indian communities has inhibited the development of traditional Indian government because elite interests are well served by the kind of political and economic system advocated by the Department of Indian Affairs. Such a system enables the elite group to conduct band affairs in such a way as to maintain and advance its self-interests. This elite group of Indians does not want its people to regain authority over their own affairs because that would require leaders to be accountable to their people. In effect, the elite class of Indians is fronting for the Indian Affairs Branch by persuading the mass of band members to accept what the Canadian government is pushing. The elite are telling Indian people that if the proposed Indian-government legislation is passed by the Canadian government, Indians will have what they want – self-determination. What they are not saying is that the systems, the institutions, the structures associated with legislated Indian government will be the same as those under the Indian Affairs Department.

In Indian communities elitism is sometimes promoted by people who go to university and return home believing they have the right, the authority, and the wisdom to tell people what they should do or what is best for them. They assume that they should hold a superior economic and social position in the community. Elitism is a European ideology and philosophy. It is completely contrary to our traditional philosophy and ideology, and it is very dangerous to the survival of Indian communities.

Reassertion of the peoples' authority is a critical issue if Indian government is to have any real meaning. The Neskainlith Indians of the Shuswap nation, whom I mentioned earlier, are doing just that. These people are standing up and challenging their leaders, asking the fundamental question: 'Who gave you your authority – the people, or the Canadian government?' They are struggling to re-establish and revitalize traditional processes of decision-making, which eliminate the danger of elitism. Without revitalization of the traditional system of leadership and of leadership selection, I foresee that Indian society will evolve into a two-class system of 'haves' and 'have-nots.'

An alternative model of government available to Indians is one that places the locus of authority in the smallest political unit. The larger, more encompassing political units would play only a delegated, *co-ordinating* function. Under such a model we would resurrect family-clan groups and band communities. Each band would select its representatives to send to the tribal council. These representatives would get their direction from their band constituents. They would have specified responsibilities and limited authority. Thus, the tribal unit would function as it did traditionally, acting only in instances where the bands comprising the tribal unit had shared concerns, but ultimate authority would continue to rest within each band community.

The next step in building Indian government would be to resurrect and reactivate the tribal confederacies to act as encompassing units in matters of shared tribal concerns, such as commerce, trade, and political representation at a higher level. The confederacies, like the tribal units, would function in the traditional manner, that is, in the spirit of specified responsibilities with limited authority. With such constraints a political unit is less vulnerable to rule by bureaucracy because the authority to build a 'top-down' bureaucracy is lacking. By vesting authority in the smallest political unit, the necessary administrative structures are kept as close as possible to the people. This increases the likelihood that they will be more sensitive and responsive to community needs than are the currently functioning oversized (Canadian and Indian) political-bureaucratic organizations to be found in Ottawa and the provincial capitals. An example of rebuilding Indian societies along the lines I have described can be observed in the Shuswap nation in British Columbia. The Shuswap nation comprises twenty-four bands united in a tribal confederation. The Shuswaps are related to other Salish groups, thus offering the potential to go on organizing into a confederation of Indian nations.

A model such as I am advocating would require a degree of communal sharing. Many people believe the concept of communal sharing is extinct in Indian communities, but I think it is very much alive. It merely hasn't been allowed to function. It hasn't had an opportunity to express itself in contemporary Indian society.

In all of this, I am detailing what I consider to be the best path to the development of an Indian political unit that can negotiate effectively with the government of Canada. We must have such a united political body because, if we try to negotiate on the basis of one Indian nation at a time, we are much less likely to succeed than if we do it as a united people. But in all of this we must be careful to honour an important traditional principle – that is, not to dictate to any Indian community how it should deal with its internal affairs. We as Indians hold many interests in common on which we can work together. We must work together on those commonalities but not involve ourselves in trying to force all our people into accepting the same solutions.

The model of government I have described offers potential advantages not only to Indians but to all Canadians. Canadians today are having serious problems with their political institutions. Consider, for example, the municipal governments' relationships to the provincial governments. These relationships are as paternalistic and bureaucratic as is the band council–Department of Indian Affairs relationship. They have similar problems of jurisdiction over resources, of indebtedness, dependence, and the alienation of people from central government. They also have the limitations that are inherent in a fragmented authority that is unable to deal effectively with the problems confronting it. Like band councils they are subject to a variety of unco-ordinated small political units (hospital boards, school boards, and so on) all beholden to a central government and lacking the authority for integrated planning that could give a meaningful sense of community to the people. Yet this municipal-government structure is now being offered to Indians as an alternative, a *better* alternative, to our existing situation.

Frantz Fanon, in writing about the process of colonization and decolonization, identifies several sequential stages and impacts upon individuals and society. While his account may be overly dramatic, I have found parallels between the stages and impacts he describes and what our people are experiencing, particularly our experience in the last two generations. Indians are currently in the stage, identified by Fanon, where we believe that we are an inferior people. This sense of inferiority is evident in the way we are negotiating the terms of Indian government with the Canadian government. There is an underlying attitude that we have nothing of value in our communities, that the good things are to be found outside of our communities, that we must have federal officials tell us what to do.

A specific example of our sense of inferiority can be observed in the prevailing assumption among our people that we have to go to university for knowledge. Yet we have our elders to give us guidance. They have no university education, but they have a lifetime of understanding and wisdom to offer us. Until about ten years ago we had very few Indians in universities, but we survived and achieved. When I worked with the National Indian Brotherhood, only two members of the executive council had any university training. Yet they were all very knowledge-able about the white man's system – not only knowledgeable, but wise about it, knowing all its traps and pitfalls.

I observe a sense of inferiority, also, in our assumption that we need hospitals and doctors to have good health. Yet the evidence shows these have not contributed to our good health. They represent only an ineffec-tive curative, not a preventative approach. Indians had far better health under the traditional system than we have today.

If we really want to help ourselves, we must revitalize our institutions. We must turn to our own traditional structures, systems, and processes. This does not mean that we have to return to the way we were two or three hundred years ago. Given our experience and knowledge about the failures of the European institutional structures, systems, and processes, why should we repeat their mistakes? Why, for example, should we adopt an educational system that not only fails to meet the needs of its students but also alienates them in the process? Yet we are currently on a course of introducing that type of educational system into our Indian communities. I believe we are uncritically adopting European-Western institutional approaches because of our sense of inferiority. We are doing it because we do not have confidence in our ability to build something that will be workable, more appropriate to our needs, and more effective. I am convinced that Indians can find in their traditional philosophies and ideologies better and more meaningful approaches than those offered by the Canadian government. We have something to offer that even other Canadians can look to as a better alternative to their existing institutions.

I know it is difficult to change institutions once they are established. This is where Indians are fortunate. We have not fully accepted the Canadian model of political, economic, and social administration and management as our own model on the reserves. We still have a chance to shape our institutions so they will conform to our traditional philoso-phies and ideologies and to adapt these to contemporary times so they will be as useful as they were previously to our community. But it is essential that Indians insist on traditional institutions, systems, and pro-cesses as the framework for any discussion of Indian government. Our traditional philosophies and ideologies are absolutely vital to our future. They must be clarified to give our people a real alternative.

My proposed approach to Indian government is not an easy route. Most things worthwhile are not easy to obtain. It will require much thought and planning. Without careful deliberation our 'solutions' will only multiply our problems. In this process of thinking and planning, we must beware of the traitors in our midst – those of our people who have already accepted elitism, materialism, and individualism, who are trying to convince us that the Canadian way is the only way. Yes, it may be inevitable that our greatest enemies are within our own ranks.

Notes

1 Under this principle all members of the community had to be involved in decision-making. The elders were involved as wise men. They counselled the younger generations. Children, too, were included in the decision-making process.
2 This section of the UN has a committee called the Committee of 24 which has been dealing with colonial, decolonization, and trusteeship matters. It has been talking as though its work is almost finished, despite the fact that Indians in many parts of the world are still colonized.

KIRKE KICKINGBIRD

Indian Sovereignty:
The American Experience

'Sovereignty' is a word that is used with a great deal of facility. Our standardized mental image of the word calls for a white-haired gentleman in an ice-cream suit with black string tie shouting in a heavy southern accent, 'The great SOVEREIGN state of Alabama casts its votes for the next president of the United States ...' The word appears in virtually every daily newspaper and weekly newsmagazine. For those who shun the printed word, the term 'sovereignty' is heard with regularity on the evening news as countries in the Third World modify political relationships among themselves and with the rest of the world. Consequently, sovereignty is displayed with a maximum of use within a variety of circumstances. What sovereignty needs is to be placed in a context that provides some meaning.

Sovereignty is a difficult word to define. It is a difficult word to define because it is *intangible: it cannot be seen or touched*. It is very much like an awesome power, a strong feeling, *or the attitude of a people*. What can be seen, however, is the exercise of sovereign powers.

Sovereignty is also difficult to define because the word has changed in meaning over the years. For our purposes, a good working definition of sovereignty is: *the supreme power from which all specific political powers are derived*. Sovereignty is inherent; it comes from within a people or culture. It cannot be given to one group by another. Some people feel that sovereignty, or the supreme power, comes from spiritual sources. Other people feel that it comes from the people themselves.

Although the modern concepts of sovereignty were formally developed and written about by European philosophers and political scientists, the ideas associated with sovereignty are part of many cultures. Throughout the world, people who live together, who come from similar cultural backgrounds, and who share common attitudes towards life feel they have the right to be sovereign. Thus, the word is used today to mean the special quality that nations have that enables them to govern themselves.

Does sovereignty mean complete independence? Again in the ideal sense, sovereignty means the absolute or supreme power of a people to govern themselves, completely independent from interference by or involvement with other sovereign nations. Yet no nation in the world today is completely independent. Our industrialized world of mass communications, global transportation, and soaring populations makes national isolation virtually impossible. Economic and political considerations, such as the need for raw materials or military assistance, make nations dependent upon each other. In reality, the economic dependence of one nation on another often leads to political limitations as well. Consequently, even such large and powerful countries as the United States and the Soviet Union are limited in their capacity to act by the small oil-rich nations of the world. This dependence has been continually demonstrated during the energy crisis of recent years.

Some people fall into the trap of equating sovereignty with nationhood, government, or politics. While sovereignty, nationhood, government, and politics are related, it is important to remember that sovereignty is absolute and comes before nations, governments, and politics. Sovereignty has the most meaning in a practical sense when we look at the sovereign powers exercised by a government. So the most basic power of a sovereign people is the power to select their own form of government.

What kind of government it is or how it functions does not affect the sovereignty of the nation. Throughout the world, democracies, monarchies, theocracies, and dictatorships all exercise sovereign powers to one extent or another. The exact methods of governing also vary widely. Some governments operate under written constitutions, others under customary or spiritual laws handed down from generation to generation. Some have highly structured institutions; others have relatively simple, informal organizations. Many nations operate under a system that allows for orderly change in leaders and powers. A change in the form or procedures of government or in one of its institutions, however, does not affect the sovereignty of a nation.

There is no magic formula about how many and which of these powers a nation must exercise in order to be sovereign. How and if a nation uses any or all of these powers is dependent on many things, including: 1 / the will and needs of the people; 2 / the history and ideology of the people; 3 / internal and external economics; and 4 / internal and external politics.

All of the colonial powers, and later the United States, also recognized the sovereignty of Indian nations by entering into over eight hundred treaties with Indians. Under international law, treaties are a means for sovereign nations to relate to each other, and the fact that Europeans and the United States made treaties with Indian nations demonstrates that they recognized the sovereignty of Indian nations.

In *Worcester* v *Georgia*, the United States Supreme Court said that 'the very fact of repeated treaties with them recognizes [the Indians' right to self-government] and the settled doctrine of the law of nations is that a weaker power does not surrender its independence – its right to self-government – by associating with a stronger, and taking its protection.' The power of Indian nations to wage war was pointed out by the United States Supreme Court on several occasions as evidence of their sovereign character. And when critics complained that Indian tribes were not 'nations' in the European sense, the court responded that:

The words 'treaty' and 'nation' are words of our language, selected in our diplomatic and legislative proceedings, by ourselves, having each a definite and well-understood meaning. We have applied them to Indians as we have applied them to other nations of the earth. They are applied to all in the same sense.

While the exercise of sovereign powers by Indian governments has been restricted to some extent, there can be no doubt that the United States and other nations have recognized the inherent sovereignty of Indian nations and their right to self-government. Consequently, we know that Indian governments are sovereign because:

1 Indians feel they are sovereign.
2 Indian governments historically exercised sovereign powers.
3 Other nations have recognized the sovereignty of Indian governments.

The distribution of governmental powers between the federal government on the one hand and the original thirteen states on the other hand was delineated in the United States Constitution. The states delegated certain powers to the federal government and retained others. Included in this delegation to the federal government was the power to make treaties with Indian nations.

The distribution of governmental powers between the United States government and each Indian nation was somewhat similar. It may be viewed as a process of dividing up a bundle of sticks. Each stick represented a sovereign power. So there was a power to declare war, a power to impose taxes, a power to regulate property, and so forth. Originally the tribe held the entire bundle of sticks and so had complete power over the geographical area it controlled and the people living within that area. The tribe was absolutely sovereign. Over the decades and for various reasons, each tribe granted certain of those powers to the United States government in exchange for certain benefits and rights. This was done by treaty or agreement or statute. The point to remember is that all of the powers were originally held by the tribes, not the United States government. Whatever powers the federal government may exercise over Indian nations it received from the tribe, not the other way around.

United States law is clear, however, that an Indian nation possesses all the inherent power of any sovereign government except as those powers may have been qualified or limited by treaties, agreements, or specific acts of Congress. Therefore, while tribes have lost some of the 'sticks in the bundle,' they retain all the rest. So they can and do exercise many sovereign powers. Included among these inherent powers of Indian governments are the following:

1 The power to determine the form of government.
2 The power to define conditions for membership in the nation.
3 The power to administer justice and enforce laws.
4 The power to tax.
5 The power to regulate domestic regulations of members.
6 The power to regulate property use.

The United States Congress has played a major role in the continuing relationship between Indian nations and the United States government. This is clear from the fact that American Indians have been the subject of more federal legislation than any other single group in the United States. Since 1790, when the first Indian Trade and Intercourse Act was adopted, Congress has approved more than four thousand treaties, agreements, and statutes relating to Indian affairs. Some of these represented good-faith attempts by Congress to deal with Indians honourably. Some were only thinly disguised measures designed to take Indian lands and destroy their governments. Many have limited, directly or indirectly, the power of Indian nations to exercise their sovereign rights.

The function of the United States courts is, in part, to interpret the laws passed by Congress and to determine the constitutionality of those laws and the legality of acts by federal officials under those laws. Therefore, laws and the actions of officials administering those laws have sometimes been challenged in the federal courts when they interfered with the exercise of Indian sovereign rights. Generally, the federal courts have permitted both the Congress and the president broad latitude in their powers to deal with Indian nations.

But while the courts have generally upheld the United States powers in Indian matters, they have also recognized the inherent sovereignty of Indian nations. The main principle that emerges from court decisions is that Indian governments may exercise all their inherent powers unless Congress has restricted the use of those powers or the Indian nations have voluntarily given up those powers in a treaty or agreement.

The courts have also developed rules for interpreting federal laws dealing with Indians that may limit interference with Indian sovereignty. For example, the courts have held that agreements with Indian nations should be interpreted in the way in which they were understood by the Indians and that federal laws should be interpreted in favour of the Indians, if possible.

Concepts about Indian sovereignty were discussed by the United States Supreme Court in two landmark cases in the 1830s. The two cases were *Cherokee Nation* v *Georgia* (1831) and *Worcester* v *Georgia* (1832). In *Worcester* the United States Supreme Court recognized that Indian nations were 'distinct political communities, having territorial boundaries, within which their authority is exclusive and having a right to all the lands within those boundaries ...' Since the Cherokee nation retained its inherent sovereignty, the state of Georgia could not impose its laws over the Cherokee nation. Instead, the relationship between the Cherokee nation and the citizens of the United States was strictly a matter between the Cherokees and the federal government. The Supreme Court statement in

Worcester v *Georgia* is still referred to in cases today in support of the inherent sovereignty of Indian nations.

Today Indian nations are sovereign and do exercise many sovereign powers. They are not mere social organizations, any more than any other legitimate governmental unit is. They are not artificial creations of the United States government any more than the governments of foreign nations are. On the contrary, Indian governments are viable, functioning political units that exercise inherent sovereign powers.

There are, of course, great differences among Indian nations in their abilities and desire actually to exercise their sovereign powers. Some have well-developed and sophisticated governmental institutions that function efficiently and exercise power wisely. Other Indian governments are in great need of technical assistance, training programs, and a stable source of funding in order to function to their full potential and serve the needs of their people. When we recognize that almost 83 per cent of all United States 'federally recognized tribes' have very small populations and limited resources, it is readily apparent that the practical problems of exercising sovereign rights are formidable for many Indian nations. There are, however, modern developments that encourage optimism and confidence in the future of Indian nations.

There are basically two reasons why many Indian sovereign powers have not been fully exercised since the early 1800s: suppression by non-Indians and a reluctance on the part of many Indian governments to exercise the powers they retain. Historically, the non-Indian attitude towards Indian self-government was influenced by the pervasive belief that Indian culture, social institutions, and governmental forms were inferior to those of European immigrants. The hope was that after enough 'education,' the Indian would realize this, abandon his more traditional ways, and embrace the non-Indian culture. This would eventually lead Indian governments to wither and disappear. As we have seen, a great deal of federal legislation throughout the nineteenth and early twentieth centuries was designed to encourage this policy. But the survival of Indian nations today is resounding proof of the short-sightedness and lack of understanding inherent in that belief and the policies it nurtured. While the belief that Indian nations may disappear still lingers in the minds of some people, there has been a growing acceptance within the United States government in recent decades of the strength of Indian nations and their determination to re-establish meaningful control over their lives and resources.

The other reason Indian sovereign powers have not been fully exercised in this century is a reluctance among the Indian people to do so. Perhaps because of a fear that the United States government will return to its policies of suppression and termination or perhaps because of an overall lack of confidence, Indian governments have not exercised many of the sovereign powers that, in law, they retain. But this also is changing. Today Indian nations are realizing that the best way to prevent interference in their internal affairs is to take firm control of those governmental functions that are crucial to their continued survival. An example of this increased awareness is the American Indian Declaration of Sovereignty adopted by the National Congress of American Indians in 1974.

The land base and natural resources of Indian nations continue to be important today as a means of preserving Indian sovereignty. Through control over Indian lands and resources, Indian nations can regain a degree of economic self-sufficiency necessary to Indian self-determination.

Until recently, the United States' Indian policy in the administration of law and order had evidenced little concern for Indian traditions, cultural values, and self-determination. The dominant law-and-order influences on reservations have frequently been either the Bureau of Indian Affairs or other federal or state entities. But recent years have shown an important trend towards Indian nations regaining control over law-and-order systems on reservations.

There are, to be certain, some problems arising with imposition of these expanded powers of self-government. Resistance by the states is the major one. Other problems are evident, such as decisions about cross-deputization of police, the question of choosing formal or informal extradition agreements, too much BIA control in ratification of governing documents, gaining the general co-operation of surrounding non-Indian governments, and a low priority in the nation itself when dealing with law-and-order matters. All these problems slow down the process of returning to a form of law-and-order administration tailored to the unique situation of each Indian community.

Indian nations have resumed the use of treaties to relate to each other in recent years. The Comanche and Ute nations are using a treaty to mend old wounds. Traditional enemies in the past, they are currently finalizing negotiations of friendship and trade between each other. In the Pacific North-West, Indian nations are currently in the process of negotiating treaties between each other in relation to the conduct and management of fishing rights in their traditional fishing places.

Even this short review should be enough to show that Indian sovereignty is a far-reaching and vigorous reality today. As a former commissioner of the Bureau of Indian Affairs stated: '[The] will for self-determination has become a vital component of the thinking of Indian leadership and the grassroots Indian on every reservation and in every city. It is an irreversible trend, a tide in the destiny of American Indians that will eventually compel all of America ... to recognize the dignity and human rights of Indian people.' He also could have added that this will spring naturally from the sovereignty of the Indian people and their tenacious refusal to surrender it.

3 Bureaucracy, Public Policy, and Indian Government

HISTORICALLY, INDIAN GOVERNMENT in Canada has operated under the bureaucratic constraints of the Department of Indian Affairs and Northern Development (DIAND). As a consequence, Indian leaders have pursued their objective of increased self-government through negotiation with bureaucratic policy-makers. Increasingly, however, Indian leaders have become disenchanted with this process. They charge DIAND with incompetence and inertia or, worse, with placing its own self-interest above the welfare of Indian people. Furthermore, DIAND is seen as unable or unwilling to understand Indian culture and aspirations.

From another perspective, however, the ineffectiveness of DIAND can be viewed as stemming from factors beyond its control. DIAND's policy-making latitude is bounded on one side by legal barriers instituted by the Department of Justice and on the other by the fiscal-restraint policies of the Treasury Board. This leaves little capacity for constructive or innovative policy-making. DIAND's impotence has affected negotiations between Indian leaders and federal bureaucrats on important issues such as self-government. Increasingly these negotiations are shifting away from substance to process, to agenda-setting rather than decision-making. Indians are reacting to this situation by changing their strategy from negotiating with bureaucrats to political activism.

In the first essay, David Nicholson, a former assistant deputy minister in DIAND, analyses the department's approach to Indian self-government. He presents evidence that negotiations between the department and Indian leaders have failed largely because officials in DIAND deviated from their own policy guidelines by neglecting to consult with Indian leaders. In the second essay, Sally Weaver contends that, despite all the rhetoric, Indian self-government is basically still at the level of a 'value-notion.' She proposes that Indians, not federal bureaucrats, must take the initiative in developing an implementable form of Indian government. Next, the editors critically analyse the latest proposal from DIAND for an optional charter-based form of Indian self-government. They hold that, while the proposal potentially implies some devolution of authority to Indian bands, it does not offer any significant change in the existing legal relationship between the federal government and Indian peoples. At best, the proposal represents a form of controlled self-government – a far cry from the political sovereignty sought by many Indian leaders. In the fourth paper H.W. Thiessen sketches some basic positions of a provincial government (Alberta) towards increased self-government. His contribution provides some insights into the federal-provincial tug-of-war over responsibility for Indian peoples. Finally, Andrew Ebona provides a comparative analysis of the problems faced by American Indians in their quest for increased political autonomy.

DAVID NICHOLSON

Indian Government in Federal Policy: An Insider's Views

To understand properly the development of the policies of the Department of Indian Affairs and Northern Development towards Indian self-government it is helpful to review briefly some historical events that bear on the relationship between the federal government and the Indian people of Canada. Indian Affairs is the oldest continuously operating arm of government in Canada. It was instituted by the British imperial government in the mid-1700s, and until 1860 it discharged the responsibility of the Crown to the indigenous peoples. After 1860 Indian Affairs was established as a department of the Canadian government. Since that time it has undergone a succession of moves within the federal bureaucratic structure. These moves have had much to do with the priorities that succeeding governments have attached to Indian matters and the Indian condition.

In 1867 Indian Affairs was housed in the Secretary of State's department; in 1936 it was relocated in the Department of Mines; from there it went in 1950 to the Department of Citizenship and Immigration; and finally in 1966 it was established as an autonomous and separate Department of Indian Affairs and Northern Development. Respectively, some of the significant events prompting these moves were the signing of treaties and the passage of the Indian Act in the 1870s; the increased interest in resource exploration on Indian lands in the 1930s; a renewed emphasis on assimilation of Indians following World War II; and the heightened concern of Indians over aboriginal rights, treaties, and resources, beginning in the 1960s.

In 1968 the department developed what is now known as the White Paper. This document delineated a policy for removing the special status of Indians under the Indian Act. Made public in 1969, the proposals contained in the White Paper established in the minds of Indian people the conviction that the federal government was openly committed to a process of assimilation, integration, and elimination of Indian peoples in Canada. The Indian response to this policy was one of immediate, unreserved, and vehement repudiation. The intensity of Indian reaction to the White Paper impelled the Canadian government to make a commitment that it would not amend the Indian Act without first consulting the Indian people. My observations of ensuing events since this commitment was made lead me to believe that the Canadian government is still deliberately and systematically committed to implementing its 1969 White Paper proposals. What follows is my analysis of the significant events that have occurred since 1968 that have a bearing on the federal government's policies towards Indian government. This analysis is based on personal perceptions that I gained during my participation and involvement at a senior administrative level in the Department of Indian Affairs during the 1970s.

The federal government's first response following the Indians' negative reactions to the White Paper was to step up its core funding to Indian associations and bands. I believe this was done primarily to assist Indians to draw the attention of the private sector and the provincial governments to their deprived economic and social condition. In 1971 the federal government approved and implemented a major economic-development program for Indian communities. In my view this initiative was taken to spur the integration of the Indians' economy or business sector into the Canadian economy. It encouraged involvement by the provinces and the private sector in providing free equity and debt financing to bands and band business operations. Concurrently with this economic-integration initiative, the federal government placed an increased emphasis on integrating Indians into the provincial educational system through negotiated tuition agreements with provincial educational authorities. The result was a concomitant reduction in the construction of federally administered reserve-based schools. Also, and at the same time, tripartite federal-provincial–Indian-band negotiations were fostered, with the goal of extending a full range of provincial social services to status Indians residing in urban settings.

In 1974 a policy paper was developed by the federal government entitled 'Indian–Federal Government Relationships.' Its principles were based on the concept of a partnership between the federal government and Canada's Indians. It affirmed that the federal Department of Indian Affairs would involve Indian people in policy formulation affecting Indians, and it set out the processes for involving Indian people in joint program development. It redefined the role of the public servants within the Department of Indian Affairs, recasting them as 'advisers' in contrast to 'managers.' One must consider this development in historical perspective: the government first viewed its relationship with Indian people as that of protector, then of manager, and today, of joint decision-maker.

At the time of the introduction of the 1974 policy paper, I had attained the position of assistant deputy minister in the Department of Indian Affairs. I was in a position to evaluate how effectively the policy of joint decision-making with the Indian people was working. It is my analysis that the process of policy development within the department never conformed to the joint decision-making model. The Policy Development Branch of the Department of Indian Affairs continued to conduct its affairs as it had prior to 1969, not by consulting but rather by imposing its policies on Indians. This approach placed Indians in a reactive role, which they fulfilled, usually by opposing government policy. I am saying that the formal process of joint decision-making was never worked out between the federal government and the Indians of Canada, although I believe there were honest attempts on both sides to make it work. The lack of that formal process and the lack of communication have contributed to many of the problems in Indian–federal-government relationships that exist today.

It is imperative, it is essential, that Indians influence the policy directions for programs of which they are the sole clients. The obstacle to this desired objective is not so much the quality or character of the people within the department as it is a lack of appropriate experience by department personnel. Very few of the policy and program developers in the department have had field experience – that is, face-to-face, day-to-day, on-the-ground, grass-roots contact with Indian people. It is difficult, even in the joint decision-making model, to design programs when you have little knowledge or understanding of the target population, in this case, the Indians of Canada.

I want to turn now to an analysis of the federal government's current legislative initiative on Indian government. The proposed legislation calls for the devolution of program responsibilities from the federal government to band governments and Indian institutions. However, in announcing this legislation the government has said very little about how the programs will be financed. Devolving program responsibility to band governments without providing the necessary financial resources will place Indian governments in a worse fiscal dilemma than the Department of Indian Affairs is in today. One hears vague references to a federal-government strategy for providing Indians with the resources so they can assume program responsibility. Apparently, one part of this strategy is significantly to reduce the 4,850 public servants in the Department of Indian Affairs, with the public-service salary-dollars thus saved to be transferred to the bands as core-support funding for Indian government. A more surreptitious part of the strategy is to force Indians to seek provincial services by holding the line on the total federal government contribution to Indian operating budgets. Because of inflation and an expanding Indian population, a 'hold-the-line' fiscal policy by the federal government will compel Indians to seek help from provincial governments or see their services reduced to intolerable levels.

Concurrently with its 'program-devolution' moves, the federal government is proposing to amend the Indian Act in order to establish a legislative basis for Indian government. It is offering to develop a charter for bands that would allow bands to accept the responsibility now held by the minister of Indian Affairs for education, social assistance, land management, and band membership. The charter would also, within limits, allow bands to pass their own by-laws. One policy goal of amending the act is to remove anachronisms and discriminatory articles from the Indian Act while adding motherhood statements about the retention of traditional culture and respect for Indian identity. Another policy goal of amending the Indian Act concerns treaty land entitlements. The Ministry of Indian Affairs has a legal responsibility to ensure that Indian entitlements to land are satisfied. Indian land entitlements are legal obligations that require the provinces to deliver specified lands at treaty time. This process will require the co-operation of provincial governments. A related policy goal of the proposed Indian Act amendment is to encourage and support the involvement of Indian people, particularly in the West, in major resource development.

The process of developing federal government policy on Indian government is significantly inhibited by several contextual factors. In 1977 the Lambert Commission was created to do an internal review of federal government operations. The Auditor General and the office of the Controller General were also involved in this review. The commission concluded that federal spending was out of control and that government departments lacked adequate systems for public accountability. As a result of this commission's findings, a directive was issued from Parliament, through the Treasury Board, setting out terms and conditions to be attached to all federal funding. This directive also applied to funds flowing to Indian bands and other Indian associations. So, while the Ministry of Indian Affairs is supposedly trying to encourage and foster the development of autonomous Indian government, it is simultaneously being forced by broader policies of government to impose stringent terms and conditions on how money will be spent, how it will be accounted for, and what systems will be put in place at the band level to achieve this accountability. These directives supersede, in a very consequential way, the implementation of policy principles for autonomous Indian government.

Another contextual factor inhibiting the development of autonomous Indian government is inherent in the very way the parliamentary system of democratic government departmentalizes its own activities. There is in place a system for funding federal departments that is referred to as the 'envelope system.' Under this system there are four major subcommittees of Cabinet: Priorities and Planning; Government Operations; Social and Native Affairs; and Economic Development. Each of these subcommittees constitutes an 'envelope' subsuming a number of government departments. Every department is required to contribute a certain share of its annual budget to its particular envelope – for emergency programs, special projects, program expansion, and so on. Then every department must compete with the others in its envelope in divvying up the collective funds in that envelope. The Department of Indian Affairs is one of fourteen departments in the Social and Native Affairs envelope. During my tenure in the government, the Department of Indian Affairs program did not enjoy a high level of prestige or influence with its sister departments. The department was seen as being inefficient and ineffective in carrying out its mandate. Furthermore, it was deemed to be staffed by civil servants of sub-average calibre. This resulted in a problem of credibility and lack of clout that made it very difficult for the Department of Indian Affairs to compete successfully for the limited resources within its envelope. Without adequate funds the concept of Indian government cannot be implemented.

As I have briefly outlined, the Lambert Commission's recommendations and the constraints in spending that flow from those recommendations are frustrating the federal government's policy initiatives on Indian government. Ironically, the Department of Indian Affairs is itself subverting its own policy objectives in this regard. During my term in the Department of Indian Affairs, Priorities and Planning, which is the senior and most powerful Cabinet subcommittee, issued a directive requiring all federal departments to develop a long-term directional plan. A key aspect of this directional plan is a statement of policy goals. During my entire period of service in the Department of Indian Affairs I do not recall officials ever consulting Indian leadership in advance of developing these policy goals. These policy goals included devolution of programs and responsibility; extension of provincial services to Indians; amendment of the Indian Act; fulfilment of treaty land entitlements; and the involvement of Indian people in major resource development. Now, once a department establishes its policy goals, the system dictates that it must prepare a document setting out the strategy to achieve those goals. It is my understanding that this strategy was developed by department officials without involvement of Indian people. The next step is for the various regional offices of the department to prepare what they call 'regional operating plans' for achieving the policy goals over a period of three to ten years. Here again, Indian people have been left out of the processes of policy and strategy development.

The federal government supports a very limited concept of Indian government. Its perception of Indian government is that Indians will exercise the powers the minister now exercises on behalf of Indians. The charter system that the federal government is proposing for bands would enable a legal foundation to be put in place to allow Indian governments to exercise those powers on behalf of the minister at the reserve level. As I understand it, the implications of the proposed federal government legislation for Indian government means this: 'nationhood' is not acceptable; 'sovereignty' is not acceptable; a 'third order of government' for Indians in Canada is not acceptable; a separate judicial system for Indians is not acceptable; a separate educational system for Indians is not acceptable; total control of the land base is not acceptable. Based on my involvement in the federal government, my perception is that there exists a wide gap between the Indian concept of Indian government and what the federal government, at this time, is prepared to negotiate and approve.

SALLY M. WEAVER

Indian Government: A Concept in Need of a Definition

During the past several years I have been keenly interested in Indian–federal-government relationships, in particular the relationship between the National Indian Brotherhood and the federal government. My concerns, therefore, are expressed from this perspective.

First, I must admit that I am confused about the concept of Indian government. Having read several position papers from Indian associations, I think the notion of Indian government at the moment remains essentially at the level of a 'value-notion.' It is as yet an unarticulated, vaguely conceptualized ideology or philosophy. It surfaced only four or five years ago as an initial idea, and, because it has not yet been defined pragmatically, a key question must be asked which may not be popular with Indian leaders. The question is, who wants Indian government? Do provincial and national Indian organizations really want Indian government? To what extent is it a serious political priority and goal for these organizations? Or does the real action and concern about Indian government reside at the local band level rather than at the provincial and national Indian-organization levels?

I see the definition and development of Indian government as a job to be done by Indian people. This task subsumes the need to define a concept of government that does not simply include the purely political aspects but incorporates the *political economy* of Indian government. I draw this observation from my analysis of the financial reality that currently contains, curtails, and shapes Indian political activism in this country. We can observe an example of this in the effect that the current cut-backs in grants to the National Indian Brotherhood by the federal government are having on that organization's capacity to lobby. As I see it, any future definition of Indian government must take into account the financial underpinnings of such a political process or structure, however it is conceived.

There are two additional reasons why it is essential that Indians themselves define and develop their concept of Indian government. First, if it were left to federal government personnel, they would put their own construction on the concept of Indian government. This process was very obvious in the 1969 White Paper deliberations.[1] White bureaucrats do not hold the same world views and values as Indians. Thus, even well-meaning government officials will attach inappropriate white values to Indian proposals. Second, in defining Indian government it is imperative that Indian leadership explicitly address the differences they perceive between what they are promoting as Indian government and Quebec's demands for 'sovereignty-association.' My research on the 1969 White Paper leads me to believe that the federal government's experience with the 'French fact' holds very negative consequences for those who want to proclaim the 'Indian fact.' The experience with the French fact has created a policy context and a philosophy inside government that bodes ill for any Indian-government initiatives.

In my work with the Department of Indian Affairs and Northern Development (DIAND) in the last three or four years, I have not detected a serious intent to transfer significant *authority* to Indians. Yet such an intent is requisite for a meaningful system of Indian government. Just as important, DIAND's powers to transfer authority to Indians are increasingly circumscribed by the strong trend to centralized powers within the federal government. I refer here to the expanding role of the Treasury Board and of the Auditor General. As power in government is centralized, DIAND's capacity to act is commensurately diminished. Furthermore, the powers currently guiding federal government policies have as their primary value 'better management' and 'greater cost-effectiveness.' Without appearing overly cynical, when one reads the Auditor General's reports and the responses to these reports by DIAND, Indians might as well be boxes of cornflakes rather than human beings and living communities.

This characterization may be somewhat extreme, but what has happened in the federal government is that the system of financing, rather than the needs and aspirations of people, has become the driving force in policy formulation. From this flows a system of rules and regulations

whose values are based on cost-benefit analysis, on conformity to regulations – basically technocratic notions. My essential point is that DIAND
has shown no evidence to date of developing an innovative people-ori-
ented policy with respect to Indian government, and even if it had, the
current framework operative within the federal bureaucracy would con-
strain it. The climate within the federal government would not be receptive or responsive to innovative notions of Indian self-government even
if the concept were fully articulated. For the federal government to be
receptive to the notion of Indian self-government it would first have to
develop a posture of wanting to be creative and experimental, and it
seems to me that ethos is just not there. What is more, within the federal
government's overall list of priorities, Indians rank very low. Of course,
Indians, women, the elderly, and the handicapped are treated as social-
policy priorities, but in terms of allocating money, Indians are far from
the top of the list.

If Indian government were to come into existence over the next few
years, it seems to me that a necessary part of the process would be a
dialogue of negotiation between Indians and DIAND. Unfortunately, the
capacity for dialogue between these two groups seems to have collapsed.
There has been a steady erosion of interpersonal relationships, and the
process of consultation often ends in ruptures. In fact, present relations
between these two groups could be characterized as those of mutual disengagement. DIAND is now nosediving into its operational and strategic
plans, and the national Indian organization is nosediving into its internal affairs. This disengagement means that the kind of climate needed for
mutually beneficial discourse and exploration of the notion of Indian
government does not exist.

From the foregoing it would appear that a formalized conception of
Indian government, as exemplified by a political-science model, is going
to experience difficulty being accepted pragmatically within the Canadian system. Perhaps Indian government already exists in the sense that
band councils are free to govern at the reserve level. If this is the case,
maybe de facto Indian government already operates at the local level and
there is no need to develop multilevel models. Realistically, I think that
the goal of Indian government will ultimately be achieved through band
governments asserting their right to govern at the reserve level. This
process will be facilitated by the development and maintenance of
stronger national and provincial lobbying organizations, representing

band interests, which can keep pounding, pressing, and monitoring the federal government. So I see a band-level government supported by provincial and national Indian organizations as being the most sensible and viable model of Indian government.

Finally, Indian leaders must view with caution the notion of entering into tripartite negotiations over Indian government with the federal government and the provinces. Having analysed the joint Cabinet–National Indian Brotherhood experience, I do not see Indian organizations as having the necessary resources to sustain such a negotiation process. That does not mean that tripartite negotiations should never be undertaken but simply that Indians must beware that their limited political resources do not get drawn into the morass of provincial-federal negotiations and thus diverted from the pressing needs of their own constituents.

Note

1 Sally M. Weaver *Making Canadian Indian Policy: The Hidden Agenda 1968–70* (Toronto: University of Toronto Press 1981)

J. ANTHONY LONG / LEROY LITTLE BEAR / MENNO BOLDT

Federal Indian Policy and Indian Self-Government in Canada

During the past several years, self-government has emerged as a pivotal concern in the quest by Canada's Indian peoples for a redefined role within Confederation. For Indians, self-government is inextricably linked to the achievement of self-determination and the preservation of the Indian cultural heritage. Not surprisingly, Indian aspirations to self-government have been tied to demands for the entrenchment of aboriginal rights and guarantees of special status in any revised constitutional scheme for Canada. At the same time, there is a recognition on the part of the federal government that the existing legal and political arrangements for Indians in Canada, in particular the Indian Act, are too restrictive and in need of reform. Consistent with this position, the Department of Indian Affairs and Northern Development has since the mid-1970s been advocating variants of a legislative-based charter system of Indian self-government as an alternative to the Indian Act. During the fall of 1982 the minister tabled the latest version of this proposal before the Sub-committee on Indian Self-Government of the parliamentary Standing Committee on Indian Affairs and Northern Development, just before the subcommittee began its country-wide hearings on the subject of Indian self-government. Under this version of the charter system there would be a devolution of federal authority over Indian affairs to Indian bands, with a corresponding increase in their autonomy.

A brief survey of Canadian Indian policy indicates that the current policy thrust towards increased self-government for Indians represents

This is a revised version of a paper that appeared in *Canadian Public Policy* III 2 (Spring 1982) 189–99.

an attempt to break away from the policy paradigm that has dominated the federal government's relationships with Indians since the beginning of Confederation.[1] This paradigm can best be described as internal colonialism, whereby the greater part of Canada's Indians have been given separate legal status by virtue of an Indian Act, have been subject to special legislative programs, and have been settled on specific land areas known as reserves.[2] In part, this policy fulfilled a perceived need to protect Indians and Indian lands from exploitation by non-Indians. But more important, the long-range goal of internal colonialism has been assimilation. This policy has been based upon the belief that social and economic advancement towards equality with non-Indians, a necessary requisite for successful assimilation, could best be achieved in insulated environments, under the tutelage of the federal government.

The most serious attempt to effect a change in the policy of internal colonialism occurred during the latter part of the 1960s when the Trudeau government, in its 1969 White Paper on Indian Policy, proposed that Indians be structurally integrated into Canadian society on an individual basis and that federal tutelage be quickly eliminated. Realizing that internal colonialism had largely resulted in the economic and social stagnation of Indians and their continued dependency on government assistance, federal officials argued that the best remedy for the Indians' problems was to give them the opportunity for full and equal participation in Canadian society. To achieve these ends, the White Paper advocated the repeal of the Indian Act, the removal of special legal status for Indians, the elimination of the centralized bureaucracy of the Indian Affairs Department, and the extensive involvement of the provinces in the delivery of social and other services to Indians both on and off reserves. Indian reaction to the White Paper was hostile. Indian leaders viewed the proposals as a design to divest Indians of their lands, their aboriginal and treaty rights, and they feared a lack of support on the part of the provinces for the preservation of their cultural heritage should their legal distinctiveness be removed. In effect, for the Indians, endorsation of the White Paper was seen as tantamount to committing cultural genocide. Faced with an entrenched opposition, the federal government abandoned the White Paper in 1971.

The objective of the Canadian government's current proposal, as perceived by federal officials, is to break out of the mould of internal colonialism by encouraging and supporting greater Indian self-determination. The assumption is that increased tribal autonomy will permit independent activity and decision-making, resulting in improved economic and social conditions among Indians and reduced dependency on the federal government. The proposal also appears to reflect an acceptance of the long-standing argument by Indian leaders that the rates of social pathology among Indians – that is, incidence of incarceration, alcohol abuse, and suicides – are in large part attributable to assimilation policies and the inability of Indians to control their own affairs.

To achieve the policy objective of increased self-government for Canada's Indian peoples, the federal government has been faced with a choice among three strategies. First, the government could choose to take no action in this area until the constitutional provisions relating to aboriginal rights have been clarified. At such time, implementing legislation could be developed or other procedures instituted that would be appropriate to whatever provisions for Indian self-government emerge from the negotiations over the meaning and scope of the aboriginal-rights clauses. Second, the government could attempt to amend the present Indian Act by removing or altering those provisions which it and/or the Indians find repressive and discriminatory. And third, the government could develop separate enabling legislation to provide for a limited form of self-government as an alternative to the Indian Act. The government has opted for the third strategy,[3] and this decision appears to have been influenced by several considerations. One consideration is the uncertainty over the meaning of aboriginal rights within the amended Constitution. If the demand for Indian self-government cannot be met until aboriginal rights are defined, years might pass before any significant degree of Indian self-government can be realized or long-term solutions to pressing matters such as discrimination against Indian women can be found.[4] Another important consideration is that the government already has authority under section 91(24) of the Constitution Act to establish a legislative-based form of Indian self-government as well as to deal with a number of other Indian demands. Finally, federal officials believe that the third approach will likely engender less opposition from the various Indian groups because, should it become law, Indian bands will have the option of coming under the new legislation or remaining under the jurisdiction of the present Indian Act.[5]

In the following section we will examine the most recent proposal by the DIAND for Indian self-government. Given that the proposal is still in the developmental stage, we will restrict our examination to key principles embodied in the proposal. Such an examination will serve two purposes. First, it will allow us to clear away some of the conceptual baggage and questionable analogies that surround the proposal. Second, it will help to illuminate impediments that may inhibit the effectiveness of the proposed scheme, for, despite the apparent consensus between Indian peoples and the federal government over the desirability of increased self-government for Indians, some very crucial differences exist between the two sides, as well as within the Indian community itself, over the form, jurisdiction, and basis of authority that any future Indian government will have. These differences must be underscored, for they reflect fundamentally different premises as to the appropriate relationship between Indian peoples and the Canadian government. Among Indian peoples themselves, the differentiated historical development, culture, and ideology of the respective Indian tribes have also led to divergent viewpoints as to the desired relationship between Indians and the Canadian government. Both the differences between the Indians and the federal government and differences among the Indian peoples themselves constitute significant barriers to the realization of increased self-government for Canada's Indian peoples.

The Federal Government's Proposal

While the precise scope and substance of the government's proposal remains to be developed, five central tenets can be identified.[6] First, a substantial part of the administrative authority currently exercised by the minister pursuant to the Indian Act will either be excised or delegated to the level of the Indian band. Second, Parliament will delegate legislative authority to individual bands over land management, financial affairs, health, education, and other social services. Third, the nature of their internal government organization and the procedures for accountability of the band government to its members will be the subject of a band constitution, presumably drawn up and ratified by members of the band itself. Fourth, Indian bands would be given the authority to determine their own membership. And fifth, the proposal would provide band governments with clear legal status relative not only to band members, both individually and collectively, but to other governments, business entities, and non-Indian persons within Canada. This latter provision would allow band governments to enter into business contracts and other forms of legal intercourse on a relative par with other governmental jurisdictions, such as provinces and municipalities.

The federal government's proposal subsumes two principles of basic importance that require examination. One concerns the authority bases of the proposal and the implications of these for the kind of Indian self-government that will emerge if the proposal becomes law. The other concerns the idea of a band constitution. The remainder of our paper will be devoted to a systematic examination of these two principles.

Authority Base

Basic to understanding the government's proposal is the recognition that any form of Indian government under the federal government's purview will exist by virtue of delegated authority of the Canadian Parliament and not be derived from an inherent right of the Indian band. Put another way, Indian government will exist by virtue of parliamentary licence. Constitutionally, the legislative proposal is based upon section 92(24) of the Constitution Act, which gives the Canadian Parliament authority to make laws with respect to 'Indians and land reserved for Indians.' All federal statutes (including the Indian Act), regulations, and allocations of monies and territories (except those stipulated by treaty obligations) are passed under the authority of this provision. Importantly, then, the intent of the proposal is to *delegate* parliamentary authority to the band level, not to *substitute* Indian authority for parliamentary authority. Clearly, therefore, the proposed Indian-government scheme envisions no alterations in the basic legal relationship between Indians and the federal government.

There have been suggestions that the model for the federal government's approach to Indian government is the 1934 Indian Reorganization Act, also known as the Wheeler-Howard Act, in the United States. Heralded as a 'New Deal' for American Indians, the Indian Reorganization Act (IRA) discontinued the alienation of Indian lands through the allotment process, provided for the establishment of reservation governments based upon tribal constitutions, and provided for limited tribal control over financial and other affairs. Theoretically, the IRA was intended to bring about meaningful self-government for American Indians through the preservation of the cultural autonomy of tribes and the resurrection, at least in some cases, of traditional political and social structures.[7] It is obvious that certain structural similarities exist between the IRA and the proposed legislation in its preliminary form. But these structural similarities conceal a fundamental difference between the IRA and the proposed Canadian legislation. That difference lies in the differing legal status of Indian tribes within the two countries.

In the United States, the principle of limited internal sovereignty of Indian tribes, which includes at least a limited right to self-government, has been a consistent theme throughout its constitutional history. This doctrine rests on two lines of reasoning. The first holds that Indian tribes within the United States represent 'domestic dependent nations' (*Cherokee Nation* v *Georgia* 1831). In an 1832 decision of the U.S. Supreme Court, Chief Justice John Marshall extended this limited notion of Indian sovereignty to include the right to self-government:

The settled doctrine of the law of nations is, that a weaker power does not surrender its independence – its right to self government – by associating with a stronger, and taking its protection. A weak state, in order to provide for its safety, may place itself under the protection of one more powerful, without stripping itself of the right of government and ceasing to be a state (*Worcester* v *Georgia* 1832).

The crux of this position is that even though Indian tribes were placed within the jurisdiction of the American government after the United States achieved statehood, they retained the basic right to self-government. This position also underlies the American approach to viewing treaties as agreements more or less on the same basis as treaties in international law.

The second line of reasoning contained in the American doctrine of limited internal sovereignty holds that Indian tribes, because of their dependent status, cannot exercise powers that belong to or conflict with those of the dominant sovereign, the government of the United States. This makes Indian tribes subject to the plenary authority of the United States to the extent that the government chooses to exercise it. Taken together, these two lines of reasoning have resulted in the legal doctrine that, while the source of Indian sovereignty is inherent in the tribe itself, it is circumscribed by congressional authority – that is, the powers of self-government of Indian tribes 'are recognized, but not created, by the United States.'[8]

The Canadian doctrine with respect to the source of authority for Indian self-government rests on radically different assumptions from those of the United States. Canadian Indian tribes have never been recognized as possessing even a limited degree of internal sovereignty either by Parliament or by the Canadian courts.[9] Sovereign authority over Indian tribes resides with the Canadian state, just as it does for all other Canadians. Historically, the relationship between the Canadian government and Indian peoples can be best characterized as one in which a benevolent sovereign has taken upon itself the responsibility to provide for the well-being of native peoples. Both Indians and the federal government refer to this relationship as a 'trust.' This is not a trust in the legal sense, however, for general trust-law principles are simply not applicable to the type of relationship that exists between the federal government and Indian peoples. Rather, this relationship can best be interpreted as a situation in which the government, as a trustee, has obligations to Indians stemming from a number of sources and is obligated to carry out these obligations in a 'trustworthy' manner.

Importantly also, the Canadian government and courts have never accorded to treaties with Indian peoples the same status as has the American government. The Canadian government has tended to view treaties as legislation or pseudo-contracts enforceable because of the moral obligations that have been created. The legal character of treaties still remains unresolved in Canadian courts.[10] Our brief examination of the respective legal status of Indian tribes within the United States and Canada demonstrates first that any equation of the current Canadian proposal for Indian self-government with the Indian Reorganization Act must be critically evaluated. But perhaps more significantly it points out that even though both the IRA and the Canadian proposal have a legislative base, in the American case Indian tribes were provided with enabling legislation to bring into existence forms of self-government to which a prior right existed. The Canadian proposal, however, will bring into existence a form of legal and political authority, vested in Canadian Indian bands, to which no inherent right has ever been recognized.

The Concepts of a Band Constitution and Charter

A key concept in the federal government's Indian-government proposal is that of a band constitution or charter. The terms 'constitution' and 'charter' have been used in a sequential manner as officials of the DIAND developed different versions of the Indian self-government scheme during the last several years. In the last version of the proposal, however, the terms are used interchangeably, presumably to describe the same thing. This ambiguous use of terminology does not appear to represent any change in the government's position, but it may have introduced conceptual confusion for Indian leaders. Whereas Indian leaders had a good understanding of what federal officials meant by a charter,[11] particularly that it has a legislative base, their idea of a constitution and what it represents differs radically from the government's use of the term in its current proposal. This difference in the way the term is used may constitute a major obstacle when the government attempts to sell its proposal to the Indian community. We shall attempt to delineate the different senses in which the two sides use the term.

The idea of a constitution is basically a product of Western political thought. In Western democratic societies a constitution fulfils the need for a set of rationally conceived and formalized rules for the exercise of political power and, equally important, for the restraint of political power. Therefore, a constitution functions as the organic or fundamental law of a nation-state that defines and circumscribes the operations of government. Most constitutions are alike in their fundamentals. They include provisions for governmental structures and their respective powers; provisions for the division of authority between central and regional political units, if the country is federal; and generally they contain comprehensive charters of fundamental human rights and freedoms.[12] With the notable exception of Great Britain, constitutions of Western democracies are written documents that have been created and legitimized through some kind of constituent process following the classic democratic pattern.[13]

Evidence exists that a limited form of constitutionalism as a basis for the organization of political structures and the definition of political roles was present in traditional Indian thought and tribal social systems.[14] The Five Civilized Tribes – the Cherokees, Creeks, Chickasaws, Choctows, and Seminoles – developed written constitutions early in American history. Moreover, as Felix Cohen points out, a number of tribes in the United States had operated under rudimentary constitutions or constitutional surrogates prior to the passage of the Indian Reorganization Act.[15] It was, however, the Indian Reorganization Act that served as a catalyst for the introduction of Western constitutional principles into Indian political thought on a broad scale. Significantly, the underlying political theory of a constitution inherited by American Indians as a result of the IRA was that of the American Constitution. A major tenet of that political theory is the conceptual heritage of the American and French revolutions: popular sovereignty, the notion that the source of political and legal authority is the people. The symbolism of popular sovereignty fitted well with Indian aspirations for self-determination. Consequently, the idea of a constitution was readily accepted by some tribes because it enhanced and supported Indian notions of nationhood and sovereignty.

A study of Canadian Indian literature on self-government indicates that Canada's Indian leaders have assimilated the idea of a constitution, particularly the underlying premise of popular sovereignty, from their American counterparts. Consequently, Canadian Indians argue that a band constitution should be the result of a constituent act by the members of that band, originating in the inherent rights of a tribe. This perception, for example, is clearly reflected in a draft discussion paper presented at the Indian Government Conference conducted by the National Indian Brotherhood in Montreal in 1979:

Purpose of a Constitution
A Constitution is a fundamental set of rules, practices and principles accepted by an Indian Government that recognizes the authority of a governing body to exercise certain powers and rights on behalf of the members of the community. The Constitution also outlines the internal and external relationships of Indian Government.
Source of Authority
The source of authority is given to the Indian Government by the people it represents. *The Constitution and the laws that emanate from it describe this authority. The source of the power lies in the people themselves.* [16]

It is apparent that the concept of a constitution or a charter as it is contained in the proposed Indian-government scheme is neither the functional nor the symbolic equivalent of a constitution as it has evolved in Western political and legal theory, nor is it what Indian leaders perceive a constitution to be. Instead, as the government is using the term, it is a delegated instrument that rests on the legal authority of Parliament. It is true that a proposed band constitution would allow individual band members to participate in determining the organization of band governments, to determine the procedures for election and recall of band officers, and to establish the methods for accountability of a band government to members of the band, both individually and collectively. But the decision to allow the band members to participate in the constitution-making process, as well as the structure of that participation, are the results of an act of Parliament, not a first-order constituent act of the band members themselves.

Substantively, of course, the government's proposal for a constitution or charter represents a significant departure from the present Indian Act, where the organization of band government is highly prescribed and uniform across Canada. Ostensibly, this proposal would allow individual Indian communities more freedom in determining the form that their band government would take, although the actual degree of freedom that will be permitted by the legislation remains to be seen.

It is highly probable that the incongruity between the view of a band constitution or charter as advocated by federal officials and what many Canadian Indians believe a constitution represents will generate problems of legitimacy for the proposed Indian-government legislation. There is little doubt that the idea of a constitution is conceptually tied in with the Indian self-government movement. For many Canadian Indians, the concept of a constitution not only expresses the internal sovereignty of the tribe; it also symbolizes their aspiration for self-determination. Clearly, the federal government's proposal does not go this far. At best it represents a half-way house. Moreover, given that the federal government will require certain prescribed provisions in any band constitution, it appears inevitable that a conflict between constitutional form and traditional tribal culture will develop for many bands. Unless the federal government is willing to accommodate the uniqueness of the Indian political cultures in band constitutions, Canadian Indians may be confronted with band governments that are largely alien to their traditional ways.

Conclusion

Within the perspective of the federal government's policy towards Indian peoples over the past decade, the proposal concerning Indian self-government should be viewed as the culmination of a policy thrust that began in the early 1970s after the federal government was forced to confront the disastrous consequences of its proposed assimilation policy, as expressed in the 1969 White Paper. In our opinion, this reoriented policy direction constitutes an attempt by the government to balance the demands by an increasing number of Indian bands for greater control over their internal affairs with a desire to retain the historic legal relationship between the Canadian government and the Indian peoples.

There is little doubt that the proposal is, in part, a response to the increased political activity over the past decade of Indian associations such as the National Indian Brotherhood and the provincial Indian associations,[17] although the demands of these groups go far beyond the present proposal. However, an equally important motive behind the present proposal is the desire to bring legislation affecting Indians up to date with actual political, economic, and social developments on the advanced Indian reserves across Canada. In their drive for increased control over economic and social development, these bands have been continually challenging the strictures of the Indian Act, through court cases, band-council by-laws, or through protest activity.[18] It can be argued that in bringing Indian policy into line with current developments on many reserves, federal officials are attempting to head off what will undoubtedly be larger and more intense challenges in the future.

Even if the federal government enacts its proposed legislation, it will still have to deal with the entry of other peoples of aboriginal ancestry into the movement for self-government. The Dene Declaration, passed in 1975 by a joint assembly of the Indian Brotherhood of the Northwest Territories and the Métis Association, stressed self-determination, nationhood, and territoriality. More recently, the president of the Native Council of Canada, the national association for Métis and non-status Indians, argued for self-government for his constituency when testifying before the Special Joint Committee on the Constitution.[19] Along the same lines, the Inuit Tapirisat 'Nunavut' proposal of 1976 recommended that a separate new territory, with full partnership in Confederation, be established in the Inuit areas of the Northwest Territories. In light of the inclusion of Métis and Inuit peoples within the definition of aboriginal peoples in Canada's new Constitution, these demands could take on special significance for future federal Indian policy as well as the relationship that status Indians hold with these groups. Indian government, such as it is, has evolved in Canada under the aegis of the Indian Act, and central to that act are legal concepts of status Indians, band, and reserve. It has been, of course, those concepts that have historically defined the differences between status Indians on the one hand and the Métis and non-status Indians on the other. Importantly, the continuing salience to status Indians of these boundary criteria may herald a conflict between status Indians and the other two groups over the distribution of government funding, with serious implications for the implementation of Indian self-government.[20]

Indian self-government, regardless of which form emerges, will only be viable if it rests on a firm economic base. Realistically, the development of that base depends on the willingness of the federal government to provide a sufficient level of funding for social services and to assist the bands in the development of their natural resources, in the creation of commercial enterprises, and in the development of successful farming operations. Federal officials acknowledge that the proposed charter system of Indian self-government will require additional funding beyond the level currently committed and administered by Indian Affairs.[21] Serious questions can be raised about the willingness of the federal government to appropriate additional monies for Indian self-government.

Two final points need to be made. First, even though Indian leaders may insist on waiting until the issues of aboriginal rights and special status for Indian peoples are settled within Canada's new constitutional scheme before bargaining seriously with the federal government over the kind of Indian self-government that is most appropriate, the importance of the proposed legislation as an agenda-setting device should not be underemphasized. The willingness of the federal government to incorporate items such as the idea of a band constitution and the notion of defined legal status for band governments within its proposal firmly entrenches those items on any future Indian policy agenda. It will become very difficult for the federal government to shift the focus of future dialogues with Indians away from these issues; by the same token, it will become easier for Indian leaders to seek clarification and redefinition of these issues, which are central to their quest for self-government. Second, Indian leaders must protect their constituency from any designs by the federal government to use its proposal for scaling down administrative activity with regard to Indians as a strategy for shifting administrative and financial responsibility for Indian peoples to the provinces. Given the current jurisdictional and financial disputes between the provinces and the federal government, if such a strategy is pursued, Canada's Indian peoples will surely be the big losers.

Notes

1 For useful but differing interpretations of past Indian policy in Canada see, among others, John L. Tobias 'Protection, Civilization, Assimilation: An Outline of Canada's Indian Policy' *Western Canadian Journal of Anthropology* VI 2 (1976) 13–30; Sally M. Weaver *Making Canadian Indian Policy: The Hidden Agenda 1968–70* (Toronto: University of Toronto Press 1981); A.D. Doerr 'Indian Policy' in *Issues in Canadian Public Policy* ed G. Bruce Doern and V. Seymour Wilson (Toronto: Macmillan 1974); Douglas Sanders 'Indian and Inuit Government in Canada' unpublished paper (1978); Marie Smallface Marule 'The Canadian Government's Termination Policy: From 1969 to the Present Day' in *One Century Later* ed Ian A.L. Getty and Donald B. Smith (Vancouver: University of British Columbia Press 1978); *Native Rights in Canada* (Toronto: Indian-Eskimo Association of Canada 1970); and Wayne Dougherty and Dennis Madill *Indian Government under Indian Act Legislation 1868–1951* (Ottawa: Research Branch, Department of Indian Affairs and Northern Development 1980).

2 Menno Boldt 'Social Correlates of Nationalism: A Study of Native Indian Leaders in a Canadian Internal Colony' *Comparative Political Studies* XIV 2 (1981) 205–31

3 See statement to the House of Commons of Mr Ray Chenier, parliamentary secretary to the minister of Indian Affairs and Northern Development, with respect to developing alternative legislation to the Indian Act (House of Commons *Debates* 2 Dec 1980, 5264). See also Minister of Indian and Northern Affairs 'Strengthening Indian Band Government in Canada' (1982) 4–8, for a discussion of alternatives for strengthening Indian band government.

4 The minister has suspended sections of the Indian Act that discriminate against Indian women when requested to do so by band councils. This action, however, does not represent any long-term solution. The Sub-committee on Indian Women and the Indian Act, established by the House of Commons Standing Committee on Indian Affairs and Northern Development, has recommended that the government eliminate sex discrimination caused by section 12(1)b of the present Indian Act. It

remains for the minister and Parliament to consider this recommen-
dation.

5 House of Commons *Debates* 2 Dec 1980, 5257

6 The general features of the proposed Indian-government scheme have
been revealed in Parliament by the minister and other departmental
officials (House of Commons *Debates* 2 Dec 1980, 5254–78). The most
detailed form of the proposal is presented in Minister of Indian and
Northern Affairs 'The Alternative of Optional Indian Government Band
Legislation' (1982).

7 For useful discussions of the place of the IRA within the history of
American Indian policy, see Frances Svensson 'The Final Crisis of
Tribalism: Comparative Ethnic Policy on the American and Russian
Frontiers' *Ethnic and Racial Studies* I 1 (1978) 100–23; and Jeanne Guille-
min 'The Politics of National Integration: A Comparison of United
States and Canadian Indian Administrations' *Social Problems* XXV 3
(1978) 319–32. See also D'Arcy McNickle 'Tribal Government and the
Indian Reorganization Act: Government by Consent' in *Tribal Constitutions – Their Past – Their Future* ed James J. Lopach, Margery H. Brown,
and Kathleen Jackson (Missoula: University of Montana Bureau of Government Research 1978); and Curtis Berkey *The Indian Reorganization
Act of 1934* (Washington: Institute for the Development of Indian Law
1976).

8 Keith W. Werhan 'The Sovereignty of Indian Tribes: A Reflection and
Strengthening in the 1970s' *Notre Dame Lawyer* LIV (1978) 24

9 For an excellent discussion of the history and current status of Indian
and Inuit government powers in Canada, see Sanders 'Indian and Inuit
Government in Canada.'

10 In 1978, an opinion delivered in an Ontario District Court in the case of
Regina v *Batisse* stated: 'It is still not clear whether Indian treaties are to
be considered basically as private contracts or as international agreements.'

11 The following statement appeared among the questions to be addressed
at the Indian Government Conference sponsored by the National Indian
Brotherhood in Montreal in 1979: 'The difference between Indian Government Constitutions and the Department of Indian Affairs Charter
Systems is that the power in Indian Constitutions rests with the people
whereas, in the Charter System, the power lies in the Charter Commission and with the Minister of Indian Affairs.'

12 For a good analysis of the distinguishing features of constitutions since World War II, consult Carl J. Friedrich *Constitutional Government and Democracy* (Boston: Ginn and Company 1950) and 'The Political Theory of the New Democratic "Constitutions"' in *Constitutions and Constitutional Trends since World War II* ed Arnold J. Zurcher (New York: New York University Press 1951).

13 Karl Loewenstein 'Reflections on the Value of Constitutions in Our Revolutionary Age' in Zurcher *Constitutions and Constitutional Trends* 191–224

14 It is questionable whether the idea of a constitution as an instrument for the restraint of political authority had any meaning in traditional Indian thinking. Before the influence of European political and legal thought, authority relationships within Indian tribes were quite different from those existing within European societies. In his study of the Central Algonkian tribes, for example, Walter B. Miller found that well-defined roles existed but the role relationships were horizontal rather than hierarchical. ('Two Concepts of Authority' *American Anthropologist* LVII 1 [1955] 271–89; see also E. Adamson Hoebal 'Authority in Primitive Societies' in *Authority* ed Carl J. Friedrich [Cambridge, Mass: Harvard University Press 1958].) Moreover, Indian tribes were never confronted with a long drawn-out revolutionary struggle for the secularization of political power. For these reasons, the need for an instrument to limit the exercise of authority did not exist.

15 Felix S. Cohen *Handbook of Federal Indian Law* (Albuquerque: University of New Mexico Press, nd)

16 National Indian Brotherhood 'Indian Government Constitutions' in draft discussion paper, Indian Government Conference sponsored by the National Indian Brotherhood, Montreal, 8–9 Aug 1979; see also Leroy Little Bear 'Some Thoughts on the Canadian Constitution and Indian Government' *Ontario Indian* IV (1981) 22–3.

17 For a first-rate analysis of the rise of the National Indian Brotherhood see J. Rick Ponting and Roger Gibbins *Out of Irrelevance: A Socio-political Introduction to Indian Affairs in Canada* (Scarborough, Ont: Butterworths 1980).

18 For a good discussion of some of the attempts by bands to acquire increased control over their activities, see Douglas Sanders 'Some Current Issues Affecting Indian Government' paper presented at the conference 'Indian Government: A New Perspective,' University of Lethbridge, 25–28 Mar 1981; reprinted herein.

19 Minutes of Proceedings and Evidence of the Special Joint Committee of the Senate and of the House of Commons on the Constitution of Canada, 2 Dec 1980, 118–20

20 For an interesting discussion of the sociological salience of special legal status to registered Indians, see Noel Dyck 'Indian, Métis, Native: Some Implications of Special Status' *Canadian Ethnic Studies* XII 1 (1980) 34–46.

21 Reported in *Globe and Mail* (Toronto) 27 May 1981

H.W. THIESSEN

Indian Self-Government: A Provincial Perspective

During the discussion and events that occurred prior to the patriation of the Constitution and during the past year, issues related to aboriginal peoples and the Constitution have received ongoing national attention. In particular, preparatory meetings for the First Ministers' Conference on Aboriginal Rights provided for under section 37 of the Constitution Act of 1982 and the conference itself provided native leaders with a unique opportunity to tell government officials and politicians from across Canada about their people. They spoke eloquently of their history and their first contacts with European settlers. They told us of their unique culture, its roots, and its modern manifestations. And most importantly, they talked of the future and of how their rights should be described and protected in Canada's Constitution.

The Constitutional Accord on Aboriginal Rights signed by Canada's leaders on 16 March 1983 began the process of defining the aboriginal rights of Canada's aboriginal peoples. The amendments to the Constitution Act that were agreed to at that time were important and will unquestionably be followed by others as further conferences take place. However, I believe that one of the most important and positive results of the constitutional process may be the opportunity that was provided to all Canadians to learn of the aspirations of native people in Canada.

In my view, native leaders described four matters of fundamental importance to their people. First, aboriginal people, whether they be Indians, Inuit, or Métis, have a strong desire to protect their distinct culture and identity within Canadian society. What native people want is a recognition of their unique role and contribution to Canadian history. They want the right to be able to practise their customs and traditions with dignity. And because culture is not static, they want opportunities for the continuing development of their cultures and languages. In sum, what native people want is to be able to be proud of their special heritage.

Second, the aboriginal people want clear assurances that those rights they have acquired by virtue of having been the original occupants of this land will be protected. In Alberta, this is especially the case with the treaty Indians, who want some guarantee that the terms of the solemn treaties they entered into with representatives of Her Majesty will continue to be honoured.

Third, the aboriginal people are seeking assurances that they will be afforded improved opportunities for social and economic parity as a people with other Canadians. In short, native people would prefer opportunities for meaningful employment rather than welfare. They want to be able to provide a better future for their children through decent education. They want opportunities to participate in industrial developments occurring in and around their communities. In general, they are asking not so much for special concessions as for an end to the discrimination and barriers that have prevented them from participating as equals in the economic life of the larger society.

Fourth, and most relevant to the general topic of this paper, the aboriginal people, whether Indian, Inuit, or Métis, want to be able to exercise greater control over their own lives and destiny as a people. Native people want the skills and the opportunities that will allow them to exercise a greater degree of self-reliance and self-sufficiency. They want a greater opportunity to determine what happens in their own communities and to ensure that what happens is appropriate from their perspective. And they want to be able to have some effect on the decision-making institutions of our society.

I believe that the provisions of the Constitution Act of 1982 and the Constitutional Accord on Aboriginal Rights have begun in a real way to address, in part, the matters I have outlined relating to the fundamental aspirations of aboriginal people. With respect to the fourth issue, that of self-determination, the constitutional process has responded quite tangibly by providing aboriginal people with an opportunity to participate in that process itself. Section 37 of the Constitution Act required that a conference of first ministers be held within one year of its proclamation. It further required that the conference address constitutional matters directly affecting the aboriginal peoples of Canada and, perhaps most importantly, that representatives of the aboriginal groups be invited to participate in the discussions on those items. Recognizing the complexity of the issues and the fact that one conference could not realistically be expected to resolve all concerns, governments have agreed to extend this discussion for three additional conferences. Moreover, in recognition of the principle of the participation of aboriginal people *as* a principle, governments have agreed to include in the Constitution a provision expressing their commitment to similar consultation with aboriginal groups prior to any future amendment of the constitutional provisions that specifically deal with aboriginal matters.

The province of Alberta, recognizing the importance of the issue of Indian self-government to aboriginal people, agreed to include it on the agenda for the next first-ministers' conference on aboriginal rights. Alberta supports, in principle, measures that are intended to increase the level of authority and responsibility exercised by local Indian governments. This support, however, does not extend to the concept of sovereign Indian nations. But in making this statement, I remain very cognizant of the special relationship that exists between Indian people and the federal government arising from the treaties and the provisions of the Constitution Act of 1867. The Alberta government acknowledges this special relationship and respects treaty rights and the federal trust-relationship with Indians. In my view, the matter of Indian self-government falls within federal jurisdiction. Consequently, I feel that it would be inappropriate for me to comment in detail on the specific matters that might be included in a proposal for Indian self-government, except to note that, even though the fundamental issue rests with the federal government and Indian representatives, it will be necessary to involve the provinces in discussions on the question of jurisdictional interface; otherwise, the aspiration of social and economic parity with surrounding provincial residents cannot be achieved.

None the less, I do have some general comments regarding Indian self-government. Since 1978, the federal government has initiated two proposals for reform in the area of Indian self-government. Both proposals were strongly criticized by Indian organizations, first, because of a lack of consultation with Indians in the early planning stages, and second, because of the possibility that the legislation might impinge on treaty and aboriginal rights. It would, therefore, appear prudent to urge the federal government to take these points into account when it is planning new initiatives in the area of Indian self-government.

I also must suggest that the federal government seriously consider the financial implications of Indian self-administration for individual bands. At present the Department of Indian Affairs is subject to very severe expenditure restraints, which, accounting for inflation, entail little real growth. The problem facing the department is, in essence, how to do as much – or more – with fewer dollars each year. In this regard, my concern is that, to some extent, the devolution of responsibility to the bands for the management of the functions previously performed by the department will also mean the devolution to the bands of the problem of fiscal restraint. The adequacy of fiscal resources needed to meet local government requirements must be given very careful study to avoid passing on to the bands, under the guise of local autonomy, inadequate financial capability. Bands, when confronted with the pressure of restraints and budgetary shortfalls, will be forced either to reduce programming or to turn to other federal or provincial government departments, which are also faced by restraint. This pressure may be particularly pronounced during the earlier stages, when band and management systems are developing and, hence, less cost-effective. Again, close provincial liaison may be necessary during that early stage.

Although the federal government has the primary responsibility for Indians, because Indians reside within provincial boundaries, certain provincial policies and programs have an impact on and are accessible to Indians. It is the policy of the Alberta government that provincial involvement should be initiated only upon the request of the chief and council as the duly elected government of the band. For example, the decision by the Alberta government to make the Family and Community Support Services Program available at the request of individual bands or regional councils was a clear indication that the Alberta government was prepared to be supportive in an area that did not affect treaty rights. Perhaps more importantly, it was based on the belief that Indian people were best able to determine the need for, design, and administer preventative services at the local level.

The attitude of the provincial government is very similar in the case of Indian child welfare. Recently, the Lesser Slave Lake Indian Regional Council, the federal government, and Alberta signed a tripartite agreement that began the process of returning the responsibility for the welfare of Indian children to Indian communities and Indian people. This attitude is, in fact, not new: through the Blackfoot Agreement, which was signed in 1973, Alberta became the first province to address this issue.

In conclusion, I would like to describe briefly the operation of Métis settlements, which are under provincial jurisdiction and which are the only form of Métis landholding in Canada. Métis settlements (previously known as 'colonies') were first established in Alberta in 1938. The existing eight settlements accommodate approximately 4,000 people and consist of a total of 1.2 million acres. The settlements are administered by the Métis Development Branch of the Alberta Department of Municipal Affairs. This is significant, as the settlements were until recently administered by the Alberta Department of Social Services and Community Health. The intention behind the move was to shift the emphasis from a social-welfare orientation to one of concern for local development at the settlement level.

Although the minister of Municipal Affairs has wide authority to administer the settlements, in fact, many day-to-day decisions are being made by the settlement associations. Very recently, the Alberta government appointed a joint committee under the chairmanship of the Honourable Dr Grant MacEwan, former lieutenant governor, to review the Métis Betterment Act and regulations. The committee's terms of reference empower it to 'make recommendations to the Minister of Municipal Affairs which would allow for political, social, cultural and economic development on Métis Settlements.'

The Indian people's aspirations to exercise greater self-control and expression is a positive development that requires the urgent attention of both the federal and provincial governments. That attention and urgency has been reflected in the most recent amendments to the Constitution Act of 1982.

ANDREW EBONA

Federal Government Policies and Indian Goals of Self-Government

People in Congress and people in state government have always referred to Indian tribes as ethnic or minority groups. That is a misperception. There are four differences that Indian tribes have in relationship to other minority and ethnic groups. Number one, there is a treaty relationship with the federal government. The tribes in the Lower Forty-eight are mentioned in the U.S. Constitution, which sets them apart from other ethnic groups in the country. Coupled with the treaty relationship with the federal government are executive orders and the various Supreme Court decisions concerning the special status of Indians. Very few other ethnic or minority groups have that sort of relationship with the federal government. Number two, Indian tribes have a reserved land base which no other ethnic or minority group in the United States has. Number three, Indian tribes for the most part are self-governing by virtue of agreements signed with the federal government, or they still retain traditional self-government, like the Pueblos in the New Mexico area. The right to self-government allows the tribe to elect or appoint its own leadership. In this regard it is no different from any state government because leaders can make the decisions for the people they serve. And number four, Indian tribes, for the most part, are rural in nature, isolated from the rest of the dominant society. This, of course, is not true for Indians who are living off reservation, but it is characteristic of most Indian tribes.

Indian economic development over the years has gone through many erratic shifts, mainly because of the dominance of federal bureaucrats in deciding what Indian tribes should do. For example, the federal government in its wisdom may decide one year that tourism is good for Indian tribes, so they build all kinds of tourist facilities on reservations: motels, hotels, ski resorts, and so on. The next year it may be industrial parks. Industrial parks were in vogue for a couple of years, and it was not the Indian tribes that decided that these were the facilities that they really wanted. It just happened to be at that time a whim of someone in the federal government who said, 'Well, we think we know what is best for the Indian tribes; therefore, we will build these facilities for you.'

Over the years a number of studies have been commissioned, some by the federal government and some by private foundations, to evaluate how these enterprises are performing. These studies indicate that quite a number of programs are failing because the federal government did not understand the local situation. On reservations in the south-west, for example, in Arizona and New Mexico, expensive industrial parks are sitting empty. The studies also identify a number of problems: location problems, such as the need for access by highway or railroad; promotional difficulties; lack of adequate technical assistance; lack of expertise in the area of management; and inadequate training given to Indian tribes in planning and developing their own resource capabilities. But at the top of the list was poor co-ordination among the various federal agencies that provide programs to Indian tribes. At the present time we have a number of federal agencies that are involved in Indian economic development: the Economic Development Administration; the Administration for Native Americans; the Department of Labor, Housing and Urban Development; and the Bureau of Indian Affairs, to mention a few. All these federal agencies are involved in Indian economic development. But there has never been effective co-ordination on the regional level or national level among these agencies in bringing their programs to Indian tribes.

Indian tribes have over the years come to recognize these difficulties. They have begun to deal with them, and now there are a number of successes in Indian country. The Blackfeet in Montana, for instance, through their own initiative, have achieved success in commercial enterprises. The Lummi tribe in Washington State decided about seven or eight years ago that they wanted to maintain their traditional cultural life-style, which emphasized fisheries, so they started a successful aquaculture project. The Hopi in California decided that the best economic-development venture for their tribe was to get involved in a shopping-centre operation that has proved very successful. This was their own decision.

A major obstacle to economic development on Indian reservations is that, although there may be millions of federal dollars going to the reservations, those dollars rarely turn over more than once within the Indian communities. Thus, they contribute little to the economic development on the reservations. Instead, these millions of dollars are spent in and contribute to the economic welfare of the surrounding communities. A number of tribes have come to understand this fact and are trying to change things by helping individual members of the tribe develop small-business ventures on the reservation. Other tribes are beginning to look at getting involved in tribal economic ventures – that is, profit-making corporations operated for and by the tribe – to make jobs, dollars, and provide needed services.

To understand the economic-development problems of Indians, we must take into consideration the historical relationship of the federal government to Indian tribes. It is a history of suffocating paternalism by the federal government, lack of management expertise, and lack of planning expertise by the tribes themselves. Today there is a change going on in Indian country. Primarily this is a change in attitude among Indian tribes as they recognize the need to get away from welfare dependence. Indian leaders understand that continued existence on federally funded programs and federally funded hand-outs is leading to the destruction of their people. The welfare syndrome has grown over the past 150 years largely as a result of the efforts of well-meaning politicians, bureaucrats, and missionaries. In his wisdom Uncle Sam told the Indian tribes, 'We will feed you; we will clothe you; we will take care of all your needs.' After 150 years of this kind of attitude and this kind of paternalistic relationship, quite naturally Indians have developed a dependent mentality.

Over the past ten or fifteen years that has been changing, and today Indian tribes are breaking through the barriers that have kept them isolated on the reservation. A number of educational institutions are making valuable contributions in this regard. Universities such as the University of Lethbridge and, in the United States, UCLA, USC, and even some Ivy League universities have set up native-American-studies programs or Indian-studies programs. When I went to the University of Washington about ten years ago, although I took psychology, sociology, and political science, I also spent a lot of time taking Indian-studies courses. Being born and raised in Alaska, I had very little understanding of other Indian tribes in the United States, let alone North America. Such programs have encouraged more young Indians to move back to their reservations, move back to their rural communities, to assist in their development. This movement is very important to the preservation of the Indian life-style.

Recently, there has been a significant change in attitude on the part of the federal government pertaining to funding of programs on Indian reservations. Perhaps this change is not aimed specifically at Indian tribes, but the current emphasis on balancing the budget is resulting in cut-backs in federal programs that are critical to the very existence of tribal administrations across the country. In response to this situation, more and more tribes are looking to the state to pick up the shortfall in funding.

Indian tribes must also begin to evaluate carefully the resources available on and under their own lands as another source of funding. When reservations were created about two hundred years ago, Uncle Sam in his wisdom decided to place the Indians on the most desolate, the most undeveloped pieces of land that could be found and that nobody else wanted. About 150 years later, however, Indian tribes and others, particularly the multinational corporations, discovered that a lot of coal, oil, gas, and mineral resources were located under these 'worthless' lands. A couple of years ago, Americans for Indian Opportunities published a 'fact sheet' indicating that at least 30 per cent and possibly as much as 55 per cent of U.S. uranium resources is situated under Indian lands. Thirty-three per cent of western low-sulphur coal and 12 per cent of the total U.S. coal reserves lie within Indian lands. Fifty-one per cent of the oil and gas on federal lands is located under Indian lands. Twenty-seven reservations are estimated to have geothermal potential. And this is just a preliminary estimate of the resources that are located under Indian lands. With so many resources located under Indian lands, the attitude of Indians towards development of resources is changing. It is ironic when you stop to think about it. Only a few years ago Indian leaders on our behalf expressed a great concern to preserve the land from exploitation. Today we are adopting the attitude that development is acceptable but it should be at our own pace; that has now become the byword in Indian country.

We also need to take a look at contributions that can be made by the organizations we have created over the past few decades. There are a number of these organizations, such as the Americans for Indian Opportunity, which was established to assist members of the Indian tribes in the identification of, planning for, and development of the resources that are located within their lands. This organization has three main goals. Number one is to ensure that Indian people receive an equitable return for their resources and are able to utilize those resources as a foundation upon which to develop stable tribal economies. The second goal is to assist tribes in protecting their natural, social, and cultural environment from any adverse impacts by energy-resource development. The final goal is to aid each tribe in acquiring the capability to manage its resources. These are the broad general goals of the organization, and it is helping tribal administrations work towards these objectives.

There are other organizations, national and regional, designed to assist Indian tribes in the development of their resources, whether human or natural. Deserving of mention are the National Congress of American Indians, the National Tribal Chairman's Association, the Institute for the Development of Indian Law, and the Native American Rights Fund, among others. These organizations, because they have experience and knowledge in resource development, have an important contribution to make to the tribes. They are pointing out to tribal administrators that better deals can be made than what the federal government, through the Bureau of Indian Affairs, has offered them over the years. Perhaps joint ventures or some other arrangement negotiated directly with multinational companies can yield much better compensation and security to the tribe in exchange for the resources that are being exploited.

These organizations can also assist the tribes in obtaining non-federal funding, which is becoming very important as federal programs are being cut back. Furthermore, there is an advantage in utilizing non-federal monies, because they come with fewer restrictions attached and involve less bureaucratic red tape. A number of tribes are already taking advantage of this opportunity to broaden their support base. They are looking to the corporate and to the private-foundation sectors to augment their income for the programs needed to serve their tribes.

Up to this point I have been dealing mainly with issues relating to Indians in the lower forty-eight states. Now I will briefly touch on Alaska natives. Alaska has been in the news lately because of the Alaska Land Claims Settlement Act. There are 70,000 natives in the state of Alaska out of a total population of 450,000. The Klinkit and Haida tribes of south-east Alaska, of which I am a member, number about 16,000. We have nineteen communities that we service throughout south-east Alaska, the bulk of them being rural communities. The central council is the tribal governing body of the Klinkit and Haida tribes. In effect we are a non-profit organization. The status of Alaska natives is very complex. In 1981 we had an annual operating budget of nearly ten million dollars and a staff of about 150. We operate programs in the area of educational services; employment and training services; technical assistance to rural communities in planning for development; and services to the elderly. We have also initiated culturally oriented programs aimed at maintaining our dances, songs, and language.

About ten years ago, Congress passed the Alaska Land Claims Settlement Act. In that act it stated that the Alaska natives would receive forty million acres of land and approximately one billion dollars, to be paid by the state of Alaska and the federal government. Today (the act was passed in 1971) only 15 per cent of the forty million acres has been transferred to Indian ownership, which indicates the speed with which the federal government moves. Twelve regions were set up within the state to handle the lands and monies, with one of those regions established to represent the Alaska natives who are living outside of the state. The twelve regions are very active right now in the identification of the resources that are located within the forty million acres of land. There are mineral resources, oil resources, and extensive timber resources. In my tribe alone, within the land that we were granted under the Land Claims Settlement Act, it is estimated that fifteen billion board feet of harvestable timber exists. There is also a fisheries-development potential for Alaska natives. It is estimated that 70 per cent of the U.S. fisheries potential is located within the two-hundred-mile limit of Alaska waters.

The Alaska natives, over the years, have been increasingly active in developing a special relationship with the state government. During the past two years we have recognized the need to work with the state because of the implications of federal cut-backs in programs. We believe that the state has the wherewithal to replace any federal cut-backs. Alaska is a very rich state because of recent oil discoveries. This year alone Alaska will have approximately seven billion dollars in surplus money available. Because of that fact, the Alaska natives are working very closely with the state for a share of that revenue. Alaska natives also sit in the Alaska state legislature. At the present time there are six Alaska natives who are members of the Alaska House and two or three in the Alaska State Senate.

In Alaska, the Rural Caucus, as we call it, which is comprised of the rural senators and representatives outside of large cities like Anchorage, Juno, and Fairbanks, literally control the state legislature. For this reason we consider it to be very important for rural Alaska natives to become more involved in state politics. In fact, the chairman of the state House is a rural legislator, and the chairman of the Senate Finance Committee is an Alaska native. So there is a great deal of incentive and activity on the part of Alaska natives to become more involved, not only in state politics but also at local and national levels. Through political involvement we have an avenue for dealing not only with economic and political concerns but also with social concerns such as racism, which is prevalent in our state. We hope to continue to work through the political process and to increase our influence in order to achieve a better future for our people in Alaska.

4 Legal, Political, and Economic Constraints

NATIVE INDIAN LEADERS tend to view Indian government as a panacea for the problems confronting their people. Self-government, as a political goal, has generated a level of emotional support among native Indians reminiscent of the recent nationalistic movements in Third World countries. Strong affective identification by rank and file is, of course, very important to an emerging political order, for it contributes to the legitimacy of new political structures. However, a high degree of emotional fervour can blind leaders to harsh realities. The papers in this section share a common theme: Indian government implies some very significant legal, political, and economic challenges. If Indian government is to become an actuality, then native Indian leaders must act with realism and pragmatism in meeting these challenges.

In the first essay, John Whyte discusses the problems that the Canadian legal system poses for the realization of Indian government. He analyses the potential implications, both positive and negative, of the new Charter of Rights and Freedoms for Indian self-government. Next, Douglas Sanders suggests that increased self-government for native Indians is most likely to occur in an incremental, pragmatic fashion, through legal and bureaucratic decisions that will broaden band legislative powers under the present Indian Act. As a case in point he analyses the Spallumcheen child-welfare by-law as a tribally initiated expansion of band authority that may prove successful.

In the final paper Rick Ponting and Roger Gibbins present a sobering and penetrating look at some significant economic, social, and political obstacles to Indian governments. They caution that the feasibility of Indian government depends on Indian leaders' ability to come to terms with non-Indian political and economic institutions as well as with the expectations of their own constituents.

JOHN D. WHYTE

Indian Self-Government:
A Legal Analysis

Introduction

The evidence of the last year suggests that provincial governments are taking the attitude towards the notion of Indian government that the claim by Indians for a greater political community is not inappropriate, dangerous, and to be resisted at all costs. It seems that provincial governments consider it entirely plausible that one of the means by which the socio-economic needs of Indians can be met is through the expansion of the political autonomy of Indian governmental and quasi-governmental institutions. Clearly, however, they do accept that this is the only means worth exploring, and many provinces are working hard to meet the needs of the Indian community – meeting treaty commitments concerning land, developing hunting policies that are clear and that recognize Indian rights, funding economic development, establishing native-staffed criminal-justice programs, and creating responsive and constitutionally appropriate systems for delivering educational and social services.

As for the Constitution and its significance for the development of Indian government, it would seem that the federal government intends there to be increased political rights for Indians. This was, of course, not the original intention of the government, and it may indeed not be the intention behind the inclusion of part II ('Rights of the Aboriginal Peoples of Canada') in the Canadian Charter of Rights and Freedoms, since the style of the section is declaratory and tautological. However, we expect that part II will have the effect of increased judicial recognition and enforcement of Indian and native rights. In addition, the inclusion of subsection 2 in section 37 clearly gives Indians and natives a forum at which claims for increased political autonomy may be advanced. Although Saskatchewan rejected completely the constitutional process that brought these proposals before the Canadian people, we do not reject the developments in the Constitution relating to Indian rights. What we think is possible and fitting within the concept of political rights does not correspond with some of the claims made by some Indian organizations, but we do believe that discussions leading to defining a new political community are timely.

Having presented that as general policy, I want now to look at the legal claims advanced to support Indian political autonomy. In this I am not speaking for anyone but myself as a government lawyer with general responsibility for considering those legal questions that may bear on developing policy. In other words, my legal analysis has not been reviewed or endorsed by those responsible for policy development in Saskatchewan.

The Content of the Legal Claim

Section 35(1) of the Canadian Charter of Rights and Freedoms states that 'the existing aboriginal and treaty rights of the aboriginal peoples of Canada are hereby recognized and affirmed.' Subsection 2 of that section provides that, 'In this Act, "aboriginal peoples of Canada" includes the Indian, Inuit, and Métis peoples of Canada.' If a right to self-government is an aboriginal right, it will receive constitutional recognition under the charter. But section 35(1) does not state whether the rights it recognizes are legal rights (that is, rights that are or have been recognized by Canadian courts). Nor is it clear whether the rights to which it refers are existing rights or rights that have at any time existed. It is timely to look at the present content of the legal claims advanced in support of Indian self-government. The content of section 35 provides that the rights of Indians are to be derived from present law. Therefore, I will discuss what legal claims there are under existing Canadian law for a legal, be it aboriginal or treaty-based, right of Indians to self-government.

The position of the National Indian Brotherhood concerning the revision of the Canadian Constitution states simply: 'Indian nations always had and continue to have the right to self-government.' Delia Opekokew writes in 'The Legal Basis of Indian/Dene/Dakota Government' that to Indian people in Saskatchewan, Indian treaties constituted certain legal guarantees: 'Indian bands are sovereign political bodies, having the right to their own political, social, economic, and cultural institutions, the right to define their own membership, and the right to enact and enforce their own laws, to wit, the right to Indian government.'[1]

This is qualified by the statement that 'Indian sovereignty continues, albeit not a complete sovereign independence, because of the respect that Indians have for their protectorate status under the Queen.'[2] An April 1980 draft statement by the Federation of Saskatchewan Indians, entitled 'A Process to Achieve the Full Exercise of Indian Rights,' contains a list of twenty-four incidents of Indian political sovereignty. Many of these items are deeply troublesome in the conflict they raise between the collective right of Indians to self-government and the rights of aboriginal individuals under Indian rule. This is a problem that represents the single biggest conceptual block to Indian political autonomy, and I plan to discuss it in more detail later in this paper.

The Origin of a Legal Right to Indian Self-government

In its 1980 draft statement the Federation of Saskatchewan Indians contends that the Indian right to self-government arises from Indians' 'historical primacy as the Aboriginal people.' It is said that long before Europeans came to North America the Indians inhabited the country as distinct nations, each of which recognized the distinctness and individuality of the others. 'National consciousness was expressed in sacred and secular mythologies, religious and moral laws, rituals, material art forms, dance, and music ... Therefore,' the statement concludes, 'in asserting their political rights on the basis of their historical primacy as the aboriginal peoples of the land, Indians of today are doing no more than is contained in the notion of nations as they have always understood it and as it is recognized in international law.'

Two comments may be interjected here. One is that the basic unit of international law is not the nation but the state, which is to say that it is not inconsistent with the spirit of international law for many homogeneous communities to be contained in one sovereign political unit. And quite clearly, rights of political self-determination do *not* attach to these groups merely because they are culturally distinct or culturally homogeneous. Second, even undoubtedly 'fully independent' states such as the Soviet Union are no longer seen by all international lawyers as free under contemporary norms of international law to violate the individual rights of their citizens. International law is now looking for a balance between respect for the right of states to self-determination and the protection of individuals within those states.

To return to the legal history of Indian nationhood, we must consider how aboriginal claims came to be recognized as part of the law of the colonies. For clearly they were. Even if the right to self-government is not an aboriginal right, at least possessory and hunting rights have been recognized by courts in many former English colonies. Two explanations of how this came to be seem to be available. One is that the common law is sometimes ready to recognize a morally compelling claim as a legally binding one. The common law of torts and contract must have been rooted originally in common morality because it has no express statutory origin. The other way of looking at Indian rights is to say that they have some status under international law, and international law has been held by judicial decision to be part of common law. (Of course, there are moral reasons why judges held English municipal law to incorporate general international law, so that the international-law theory is a roundabout way of saying that Indian positive legal rights are based in morality and not positive legal sources.)

Of course the courts that have recognized aboriginal rights have done so partly on the basis of European historical practices, not just on the judges' own sense of morality. And European practice was in turn based not just on morality but on practical considerations. Chief Justice Marshall of the United States Supreme Court wrote that the Indians were 'necessarily considered in some respects as a dependent, and in some respects as a distinct people, occupying a country claimed by Great Britain, and yet too powerful and brave not to be dreaded as formidable enemies.' If aboriginal rights were recognized, it was partly because it was good diplomacy.

Professor Brian Slattery of Osgoode Hall Law School at York University, formerly of the College of Law at the University of Saskatchewan, has prepared a valuable analysis of several decisions of courts in former English colonies to recognize aboriginal rights.[3] Especially interesting is the analysis of Chief Justice Marshall's views in a pair of cases, *Johnson* v *McIntosh* in 1823[4] and *Worcester* v *Georgia* in 1832.[5] According to Chief

Justice Marshall, sovereignty over land in the United States is in the United States government. Whether that is in accordance with the abstract principles of justice or not, says Marshall, it is the law of the United States, and a United States judge cannot question it. But Marshall finds that British colonial and American practice was to recognize that, while ultimate sovereignty over land is in the state, Indians had a possessory right to lands they occupied. Only the state could remove it, not any individual citizen. In other words, without state sanction, Indians had a positive right to continue their use of the land.

The official government response to Indian claims in Canada is often to characterize whatever aboriginal rights exist as merely usufructuary. Indians can, perhaps, hunt or fish on land, but they have no right to govern themselves on it. But Marshall's judgment suggests the existence of rights greater than mere usufructuary rights. In his judgment he recognized the presence of Indian customs that determined occupation rights prior to any intervention by the state. The Indian custom was not one of individual ownership of discrete plots of land but one in which the right to control access and use of the land was determined by a community leader or by a class of leaders. Indeed, part of Marshall's judgment in *McIntosh* rests on the fact that when the Indian nations who occupied the land made a peace treaty with the United States, they transferred the land to the United States without any reservations with respect to any other individual Indian's interests. In other words, a decision by the leaders who signed the treaties determined for all purposes the possessory rights to the land. Indian leadership engaged in a political act that produced a legal effect. Hence Indian rights to land under the Marshall theory are far more than English common-law rights such as a *profit à prendre*, or some other limited right vested in a particular individual. At the very least, the access and use of the land was often governed by an Indian nation, not by individual Indians. So Marshall was necessarily endorsing at least a limited right of self-government. And it is hard to find a logical explanation of why the right to self-government should be limited to land management. If Indians had a right, by virtue of their nationhood, to manage the lands they occupied, why should they not also have the right to manage other aspects of their community life?

The Indian claim to a right to self-government is often backed up by reference to the Proclamation of 1763. For example, Delia Opekokew in her paper states: 'The Royal Proclamation of 1763 confirmed the aboriginal rights of Indian people by consolidating the treaty-making process for all future transactions between Indians and the Crown.'[6]

Whether the proclamation actually applies to Saskatchewan or not, it is considered a statement of the British policy towards Indians. It provides that lands in specified territories are to be reserved to the Indians as their hunting grounds, and they are not to be molested there. The Indian claim to self-government can be bolstered by the fact that the Indians are referred to in terms of 'Tribes or Nations' and that no provision is made in the proclamation for the government of the reserves. It might be argued from this that the proclamation contemplates that Indians will continue to govern themselves in their so-called 'hunting lands.'

Treaty Rights

The aboriginal rights recognized at common law and confirmed in the royal proclamation gave rise to the need for treaties to effect a surrender of the Indians' interest in land so that the land could be opened up for settlement.

There are seven treaties (Numbers 2, 4, 5, 6, 7, 8, and 10) that affect Indians in Saskatchewan. They were signed by the Indian chiefs and representatives of the government of Canada between 1871 and 1906. There is some variation in the language of the individual treaties, but essentially they contain three basic terms: 1 / The Indians surrendered to the government of Canada all their rights, titles, and privileges whatsoever to the lands covered by the treaty. 2 / The Indians were given the right to hunt, trap, and fish throughout the territory covered by the treaty except on tracts required 'for settlement, mining, or other purposes.' 3 / The government of Canada was to provide reserves for those bands desiring reserves, the area being based on population. The reserves were to be chosen by a nominee of the superintendent-general of Indian Affairs after 'consulting' with the Indians concerned. Other rights provided for in the treaties included annuities; tools, animals, and seed for cultivation; ammunition and twine for hunting and fishing; and schools on reserves. Some treaties provided for a medicine chest to be kept at the house of each Indian agent.

The treaties do not include any grant of political power to the Indian tribes. Although there is no express surrender of any powers of self-government that might have been enjoyed, the Indians promised to obey and abide by the law and to assist the officers of Her Majesty in bringing to justice any Indian offending against the treaty or the laws in force in the territory surrendered. At the same time, there is in the form of the treaties (the bands were represented by chiefs and headmen chosen by the Indians 'in open council') and in the very act of treaty-making (which implies the existence of a separate people capable of being responsible in their political character for any violation of their promises) some recognition of the Indian tribes as independent political entities.

It is sometimes argued that if the treaty-making process acknowledged an Indian political entity at all, the substantive jurisdiction of that entity was only with respect to property ownership. That is, the process may have acknowledged an Indian right to self-government with respect to property rights, but it did not imply a right to self-government with respect to anything else. However, as suggested above in connection with the Marshall view, this theory of a limited political entity is intrinsically suspect. It seems to make more sense to understand Indian collective rights with respect to land as one incident of their nationhood rather than the full extent of it for legal purposes. It is not as though other matters were more important than land ownership and so less suitable for group decision or by some other process. Nor is it the case that Indian land rights are identical in form to ordinary English common-law property and therefore capable of ready recognition by courts. Chief Justice Marshall held that Indian custom determines the nature of the property rights. If Indian custom is that the group leadership determines how the land is to be used and whether it is to be alienated, there is a right in any individual Indian that has no parallel in English common law. Furthermore, the treaty-making process did not deal solely with proprietary matters. It involved medical treatment and education as well. And it concerned political autonomy, in that the Indian leaders agreed on behalf of their people that they would respect the laws of Canada.

Constitutional Recognition of Rights

The treaties do involve an undertaking by the Indians to respect the laws of Canada. The theory of aboriginal rights explained earlier in this talk does not say otherwise. It is admitted that whatever aboriginal rights exist are subject to the supervening authority of the federal government. So the treaties do not in themselves scuttle the idea of Indian self-government as an aboriginal right. They merely state a constraint on Indian nationhood that already existed. Or they at least state part of it. I am sure that many Indians would maintain that in exercising its supervening authority over Indians under section 91(24), Parliament is morally bound at present to have a compelling reason for interfering in Indian affairs and must respect as far as possible Indian rights. This suggests a way of understanding section 34 of the new charter. Perhaps what that section means is that Indians have a prima facie right to self-government (among other things), which Parliament can intrude upon under section 91(24) as long as it has a demonstrably justifiable purpose in doing so.

If section 1 of the Canadian Charter of Rights and Freedoms is applied to section 35 (the one dealing with aboriginal rights), we could have a solution to interpreting section 35. Section 1 provides that the rights and freedoms guaranteed in the charter are subject to 'such reasonable limits prescribed by law as can be demonstrably justified in a free and democratic society.' If those words are applied to section 35, it would mean that aboriginal rights are recognized and could only be taken away by legislation that meets the 'demonstrably justified' test of section 1. This would be in accord with the foregoing analysis of aboriginal rights: rights must be respected unless expressly derogated from by a Parliament that has a good reason for doing so. The charter would allow the courts to verify whether Parliament really had a good reason for limiting the prima facie aboriginal rights. (At present, the only limitations on parliamentary incursions into Indian rights are moral and political rather than judicial.)

This proposed effect of sections 1 and 35 would be a happy solution, but, unfortunately, if section 1 does not apply to section 35, that could mean that aboriginal rights continue to have their present status; they are prima facie rights, which Parliament in its discretion can abridge. This would, of course, give aboriginal rights much less judicial protection than other rights. On the other hand, the isolation of section 35 may mean that aboriginal rights are the most strongly entrenched; Parliament cannot interfere with them even if it has a demonstrably justified reason for doing so. The latter interpretation will not seem particularly attractive to judges. We know that they will not want to strike down a morally justifiable intervention in Indian affairs on the basis of absolute aboriginal rights. We can predict with some certainty that judges will avoid this problem simply by denying the existence of various aboriginal rights.

Limitations on the Right to Self-government

Perhaps the courts will, as a matter of constitutional construction, without explicit textual direction, infer a 'demonstrably justifiable' limitation on section 35. American courts have a long tradition of developing tests to limit the absolute language of constitutional guarantees – for example, the 'clear and present danger' justification for denying free speech, and the 'compelling state interest' test for allowing racially discriminatory legislation or limitations on freedom of religion. Indeed, this third or middle course seems the most satisfactory on its merits and most consistent (I would submit) with the existing legal status of aboriginal rights. On the assumption that the third course will be chosen (or the existing law of aboriginal rights will continue), the next task for the legal theoretician is to work out a theory of when parliamentary limitations on aboriginal rights are justified.

In particular, let us look at the potential aboriginal right to self-government. The first justification to be advanced for parliamentary interventions that interfere with Indian political autonomy is protection of the rights of third parties. If Indian decisions adversely affect members of the general population, Parliament must act to protect the general public. Thus, if measures against dangerous hunting are not taken by a band government and this threatens the safety of persons outside the reserve, Parliament would seem to have the moral right to intervene to protect the persons outside the reserve. If Indian hunting practices are threatening an endangered species, Parliament would have the moral right to stop those practices to ensure that future generations of Canadians or other states enjoy the economic and aesthetic benefits of the continued existence of that animal.

A second justification for limiting Indian political autonomy would be to protect the general human rights of members of the Indian political community who cannot protect themselves by participating in politics or by opting out of the political community. An Indian child on a reservation will have no say in Indian education policy and no opportunity to leave the reservation if he does not like it. Yet he will suffer the most if his schooling is inadequate. The state would have the moral right to intervene to ensure adequate education for all Indian children.

A third justification for limiting Indian political autonomy would be to protect other aboriginal rights. Consider the circumstances of the case of *Attorney-General of Canada* v *Lavell*,[7] where a band council attempted to expel a woman for marrying a white man. The band had a legitimate reason for doing so; it wanted to protect its cultural identity. But the woman had a claim to continue her status as a member of the Indian political community as part of her individual aboriginal rights. Perhaps *Lavell* itself is not a case where the state would be justified in overriding the decision of the Indian government. But in some cases this category of justification would certainly be appropriate.

There is a fourth possible justification for state intervention, and it is the most controversial. It is that a state measure is necessary to promote the welfare of the Indians themselves – in another, and loaded, word: paternalism. Thus the government may want to ban the sale of alcohol on a reservation even though a majority of band members favours its continued availability. Governments take paternalistic measures with respect to the general public – they impose seat-belt legislation, prohibitions on the taking of drugs, and so on. By 'paternalism' in the general context, I refer to legislation that considers an individual's own welfare more important than respect for his freedom of choice. In the context of Indians, the term refers to legislation that considers the Indians' own welfare more important than their collective freedom of choice. It is too facile to condemn categorically paternalistic measures in either the general context or the Indian context. But in the context of Indians, this much can be said: courts should be very careful about sustaining the claim that white legislators know what is good for Indians better than the Indians themselves. There should be a presumption that the Indians are most knowledgeable and concerned about their own welfare.

The case of *Jack* v *The Queen*[8] is an interesting exploration of the problems of sorting out what considerations override aboriginal rights. A 'conservation' argument was advanced to limit what appeared to be a constitutionalized fishing privilege. (This privilege was not, however, recognized in the majority judgment of Chief Justice Laskin.) This argument could be supported by the first and fourth of the four considerations presented above. Overfishing by Indians would adversely affect the rights of other fishermen, but more important, it would seriously threaten the interests of the Indians themselves.

In an opinion in which he concurs with the result reached by that majority of the Court, Mr Justice Dickson develops a promising approach to problems of Indian rights. It is receptive to native claims and sensitive to limitations inherent in those claims and moral claims that compete with it. This was his analysis of the competing claims:

Article 13 of the *Terms of Union* does not demand of the federal government 'a policy the same as that hitherto pursued,' but only 'a policy as liberal as that hitherto pursued.' That not only introduces an element of flexibility, but also requires the court to balance the pre-Confederation policy with the current measures ... Article 13 does not deprive the federal government of all regulatory authority, nor does it require an absolute priority be given to the Indian fishery.

Conservation is a valid legislative concern. The appellants concede as much. Their concern is in the allocation of the resource after reasonable and necessary conservation measures have been recognized and given effect to. They do not claim the right to pursue the last living salmon until it is caught. Their position, as I understand it, is one which would give effect to an order of priorities of this nature: i / conservation; ii / Indian fishing; iii / non-Indian commercial fishing; or iv / non-Indian sports fishing; the burden of conservation measures should not fall primarily upon the Indian fishery.

I agree with the general tenor of this argument. Article 13 calls for distinct protection of the Indian fishery, in that pre-Confederation policy gave the Indians a priority in the fishery ... If there are to be limitations upon the taking of salmon here, then those limitations must not bear more heavily upon the Indian fishery than the other forms of the fishery. With respect to whatever salmon are to be caught, then priority ought to be given to the Indian fishermen, subject to the practical difficulties occasioned by international waters and the movement of the fish themselves. But any limitations upon Indian fishing that are established for a valid conservation purpose override the protection afforded the Indian fishery by article 13, just as such conservation measures override other taking of fish.[9]

This reasoned approach of recognition of both constitutional rights, necessarily expressed in broad language, and of necessary limitations of those rights, grounded in valid state interests, is equally available as an analytical technique by which Indian self-government rights may be recognized without destroying other significant constitutional ordering principles.

Notes

1 Paper prepared for the Federation of Saskatchewan Indians, January 1980, p 1. This paper and other FSI position papers on Indian government have been rewritten and published in Delia Opekokew *The First Nations, Indian Government and the Canadian Confederation* (Saskatoon: Federation of Saskatchewan Indians 1980).
2 Ibid
3 *Ancestral Lands, Alien Laws: Judicial Perspectives on Aboriginal Title* University of Saskatchewan Native Law Centre Studies in Aboriginal Rights no 2 (Saskatoon 1983)
4 21 U.S. 543 (U.S. Supreme Court 1823)
5 31 U.S. 350 (U.S. Supreme Court 1832)
6 Opekokew 'The Legal Basis of Indian/Dene/Dakota Government' p 4
7 (1978) 38 DLR (3d) 481
8 (1979) 100 DLR (3d) 193
9 Ibid, pp 207–8

DOUGLAS E. SANDERS

Some Current Issues Affecting Indian Government

The federal government has been trying to amend the Indian Act for about nineteen years. There are four specific areas for amendment that have been discussed over the last few years: 1 / the membership system, and, in particular, section 12(1)b; 2 / land management; 3 / Indian government; and 4 / education.

The Indian Act has been impossible to amend politically in spite of repeated federal-government pledges to move on the issue of section 12(1)b. The problems of amending the Indian Act are not unique. There have been similar problems faced by the federal government in enacting new competition legislation and a new young-offenders bill. The present federal government has indicated its intentions to proceed with Indian-government legislation, but there is nothing close to a consensus on the questions of Indian government or membership. As I understand the position of the Indian organizations, there is no interest in bargaining with the federal government over Indian-government legislation. The federal government has made modest proposals on Indian government. The Indian leadership has been talking in much more sweeping and symbolic terms. There are major differences both in substance and in style.

I think legislative change is quite unlikely at the moment. If that is true, immediate change will have to come from the courts, from government administration, or from Indian governments themselves.

The events surrounding the Spallumcheen child-welfare by-law raise a number of the current issues very well. But first let me provide a context for my analysis of the key elements raised by this by-law. The issue of Indian child-care has been a recurring one in Canada and the United

States, certainly for as long as I have followed Indian matters. A major case challenging the constitutional competence of provinces to handle Indian child welfare went to the Supreme Court of Canada in 1976.[1] As a test case it was clearly one that could not be won. The facts were bad. It was conceded by all that the natural parents had so badly mistreated the child that it could not be returned to them. As well, the case was not planned as a test case. A maverick trial judge, not the Indian band or the lawyers involved, turned it into a test case. The case alleged that the province had no power over Indian child welfare, but it did so in a situation where there was no alternative child-welfare system asserted by the federal government or by the Indian band. Literally, it was the provincial system or nothing, as far as the court could see. It was easy to predict that that kind of a test case would lose.

Among those who follow Indian questions, there has been widespread agreement that the existing Indian child-welfare arrangements work badly. There have been periodic specific controversies that have embarrassed particular provincial governments. The controversies have not built upon each other, so there has been no development of political momentum to the point where there was likely to be substantive reform.

The Indian Child Welfare Act was passed in the United States in 1978, one of only two innovative statutes that came out of the work of the Indian Policy Review Commission. The act gave Indian tribes and Indian tribal courts major responsibility for child-welfare matters. Information on this legislation has circulated in Canada, but to my knowledge no group in Canada has actually made a proposal for similar legislation. In fact, it seems arguable that the Department of Indian Affairs has responded more effectively to the possibility of change than have the Indian organizations. Dr Katie Cook's research unit in the Department of Indian Affairs commissioned a study on the question of jurisdiction over Indian child welfare. As well, the Department of Indian Affairs has launched a pilot project to study Indian child welfare in the province of British Columbia. The Canadian Indian Lawyers' Association has held two workshops dealing with the question of Indian child welfare, with speakers from the United States explaining the new U.S. arrangements each time. That initiative has not, however, been picked up by other Indian organizations.

In this general milieu, Chief Wayne Christian and the small Spallum-cheen Indian band in British Columbia faced an application by the provincial superintendent of Child Welfare for permanent custody of yet another of their children. Christian himself had been raised in a foster home. His band had an unusually high number of children in care. It seemed that almost a generation of their children had been taken away. Christian, working with the staff lawyers of the Union of British Columbia Indian Chiefs, prepared a child-welfare by-law for the band and planned to enact it before the hearing on custody. The by-law is bilingual. It is written in both Shuswap and English. It is the first Indian by-law that anyone seems to know of that has been enacted in an Indian language.

The Indian Act does not explicitly give Indian bands legislative power over child welfare. As well, the Indian Act does not contain any notion that the bands have any inherent jurisdiction arising out of their original sovereignty. The assumption appears to be that Indian band councils, like normal municipal or city governments in Canada, have no more jurisdiction than is clearly given to them by legislation. To my knowledge, the idea that band councils may be different, that is, that they may retain elements of original sovereignty or have some inherent jurisdiction, has not even been argued before a Canadian court. It would be an important argument in favour of the Spallumcheen child-welfare by-law.

The child-welfare by-law was a clear innovation. By the Indian Act, band-council by-laws are invalid if they are disapproved by the minister of Indian Affairs (see section 82). That was the first hurdle for the by-law. The second hurdle would be the courts.

Mr Munro, the minister of Indian Affairs, indicated that he would allow the Spallumcheen by-law to stand. This was in no sense a statement by the minister or by the Department of Indian Affairs that the by-law was valid. The minister was saying that the department would not stand in the way of the band but that the band would have to defend the by-law itself if there was a challenge in the courts. In spite of the promise by Mr Munro to allow the by-law to stand, his deputy, Mr Paul Tellier, acting without having consulted the minister, disallowed the by-law. Clearly, the legal advice the Department of Indian Affairs was getting was that the by-law was beyond the powers of the band council.

It must be understood that there is an institutional bias against innovation in legal advice. It is safer for the lawyers (and for the doctors) to give gloomy predictions. Anyone active on the Indian scene, including the ministers and the top bureaucrats, regards the Department of Justice as a major conservative obstacle to getting things done. In this case the Department of Indian Affairs received a negative opinion from the Department of Justice, and the by-law was disallowed. But the legal decision and the political decision of the minister were in conflict. Mr Munro was forced to tell the Spallumcheen band to re-enact its by-law, and he promised that it would not be disallowed the second time around. The by-law was re-enacted and has not been disallowed. The band had successfully overcome the first obstacle.

The second obstacle was the courts. The Spallumcheen band was now ready to oppose the application of the superintendent of Child Welfare of British Columbia for permanent custody of the child. The court case, which was risky, was avoided by politicizing the issue. Chief Wayne Christian, with the support of the Union of British Columbia Indian Chiefs, organized the Indian Child Caravan, which brought a caravan of Indian people to Vancouver and involved a demonstration on the front lawn of the fashionable home of the provincial minister of Human Resources. The minister denied accusations that the province was 'stealing' Indian children and then agreed to return the Spallumcheen children who were currently in provincial care to the custody of the band council.

This was not a principled resolution of the broader issues. It did respond to the squeaking wheel quite successfully. Indian child welfare is no longer featured in the newspapers in Vancouver as a current issue. The minister's decision meant that the application for permanent custody that had started the Spallumcheen actions was dropped, leaving the Spallumcheen by-law in place and unchallenged. The by-law can probably remain in place for a few years before another challenge. In that time, the by-law could become the basis for an established local pattern of Indian child care that will have been supported to some degree by the governments of British Columbia and Canada. If that happens, psychologically, the case for upholding the by-law is strengthened.

An important part of the new arrangement is that some of the federal funds that would go to the provincial government for Indian child care will now go to the Spallumcheen band for their program. This is crucial to the long-term success of the initiative, but I do not know if it is firmly in place at the present time.

I would like now to comment on three elements that are involved in the story of the Spallumcheen Indian child-welfare by-law. I would like to comment on the scope of band by-law powers, on the issue of the application of provincial laws on reserves, and on the question of band assumption of powers. Before the last two years, the only reported court case in Canada dealing with a band by-law was an Alberta decision[2] dealing with the power of bands to make by-laws concerning trespass. The court ruled that a band could not define what constituted trespass. Since the Indian Act specified the penalties for trespass, the decision effectively wiped out band by-laws under section 81(p) of the Indian Act.

Over the last couple of years there have been cases in New Brunswick and British Columbia on band by-laws relating to fishing. While provincial hunting laws do not apply on reserves, federal fishing can apply. The question arose whether a band could oust federal fisheries law by enacting its own by-laws under section 81(o), which gives the band power over the 'preservation, protection, and management of fur-bearing animals, fish, and other game on the reserve.' A provincial judge in British Columbia has said that a band by-law under this power would have precedence over federal fisheries law. Since a band by-law did not exist in that particular case, the Indians were convicted. However, the New Brunswick Court of Queen's Bench, Trial Division,[3] has rejected any band jurisdiction over fishing, thereby effectively invalidating parts of section 81(o) of the Indian Act. There will undoubtedly be more litigation on this issue.

A second issue is the degree to which provincial laws are excluded from application on reserves. There have now been three major cases decided by the Supreme Court of Canada on the application of provincial laws. The *Natural Parents* decision in 1976 ruled that the provincial adoption laws applied to status Indian children, at least in the absence of any provisions on adoption in the Indian Act.

The *Cardinal* decision[4] in 1973 ruled that a provincial law controlling the sale of wild meat applied to an Indian on a reserve in Alberta. Legally the decision was very narrow. It turned on an interpretation of specific wording in the Natural Resources Transfer Agreement of 1930, but the majority strongly rejected what they called the 'enclave' theory. It had been argued in sweeping terms that no provincial laws applied on reserves. That was rejected with rather imprecise language, which some courts have since interpreted to mean that virtually all provincial laws apply on reserves.

In the *Four B* case,[5] decided in December 1979, the Supreme Court of Canada applied provincial labour-relations laws to an Indian-owned company located on a reserve that was receiving grants and loans from the Department of Indian Affairs and that was employing mostly Indians.

All three cases applied provincial laws. In all three cases there was no provision in the Indian Act for the particular matter, so the normally applicable provincial law was applied. This parallels a phenomenon observed for many years in the United States. The courts will fill in a vacuum. If there is no federal Indian legislation on the question and no band or tribal law on the question, then state or provincial law will apply. In at least the *Natural Parents* and *Four B* cases, the results could be reversed by changes to the Indian Act. Because that is true, the best statement of the legal situation at the moment is the statement of Mr Justice Cairns of the Alberta Court of Appeal[6] that section 91(24) of the British North America Act gives the federal government the power to make reserves enclaves. Alone it does very little. It can be meaningful, but only if the federal government uses the powers it is given by the section.

We face at the present time legislation on the degree to which Indians can control economic development on surrendered Indian reserve lands. A couple of years ago the Alberta Appeal Court ruled that provincial builder's-lien legislation would apply to an Indian-owned company proceeding with a development on surrendered Indian reserve lands.[7] Again, we had a situation in which a form of security, common under provincial law, was made to apply on reserve lands in the absence of any provision under the Indian Act on the same question. A number of these questions have now been referred to the Alberta Court of Appeal in a constitutional reference that has arisen out of economic-development plans on the Enoch Reserve near Edmonton.[8]

Finally, I would like to turn to the question of band innovation. To what degree are Indian bands able to assume authority in relation to on-reserve matters? There are clearly some areas where bands have gone their own way. The Indian Act provides a system for internal land holdings on a reserve by band members. Yet it is common on the prairies for Indian bands to ignore those provisions completely. For example, the land-holding system on the Blood Reserve has been created and maintained by the band itself without reference to the Indian Act provisions. Bands frequently ignore the Indian Act provisions that control the residency of non-members on the reserve. It has been common for Indian women who have lost status by marriage to return to their reserves, with their children, upon the death of their husbands or upon a separation. It is common across Canada for such women to be permitted to remain on the reserve, although they have no legal right to be there. The federal government will not institute eviction proceedings under section 31 of the Indian Act unless requested to do so by the band council. The band council can, therefore, effectively control their residency. The Six Nations band in Ontario has formalized this power and issues permits to individual people to reside on the reserve, a power it exercises in relation to non-status Indian women and in relation to certain non-Indians, such as clergymen.

There are a number of questions that arise about the structure of band councils. The regulations under the Indian Act require that a person must be ordinarily resident on the reserve and a member of the band in order to vote. It is common for bands to permit all band members to vote, whether or not they are ordinarily resident on the reserve. This has created some instability in relation to local government by giving grounds for challenging elections. I understand that the most common basis for challenge is the allegation that non-residents have voted. In the Northwest Territories there are examples of non-members being allowed to vote and even at least one example of a non-member being elected as chief.

By the Indian Act there are two forms of local government. The first is one established pursuant to the act and the regulations. The second is a 'traditional' form of government. The original scheme was that Indians with traditional forms of government would progress to an elected band-council system. It was supposed to be a one-way street, but that was not written into the act. We have examples over the last few years of bands reverting to a 'traditional' system. The Department of Indian Affairs has interpreted a 'traditional' system to be any system other than the system specified in the act and the regulations. In other words, if you wish to extend the term of office of the chief and council for an additional year beyond what is prescribed in the act and regulations, you may convert to a 'traditional' form of government and put that change into force. The Squamish band in British Columbia have a system of 'life chiefs' who are elected into office. This is neither traditional, in the ordinary sense of the word, nor is it found in the Indian Act.

The result of the Indian Act provisions for traditional governments is that the band can, if it wishes, draw up its own constitution which will determine its form of local government. This will not change the powers of the band council under the Indian Act. It will only affect the structure of reserve-level government.

Older Indian leaders remember that bands had some control over membership before the Indian Act changes in 1951. With the 1951 provisions we moved to an extremely rigid system. Local decision-making was virtually wiped out, except in situations where individuals applied to transfer from one band to another. The main consequence of Indian status under the Indian Act is the ability to live on a reserve. As I have indicated, band councils in fact exercise the power to permit non-members to reside on reserve land. In this way bands have assumed something of the practical power to determine questions of membership. Many bands have taken over the administration of their own membership system, but, according to the Department of Indian Affairs, their task is limited to applying the rules found in the Indian Act and elaborated on by the registrar in Ottawa. The band simply becomes an arm of the central decision-making system on membership. As the role of local band administration grows, we are approaching a situation in which the band can fairly easily stand between the data and the Department of Indian Affairs. What would the department do if the band collectively decided to run its own membership system and individual members and band council ceased to deal with the Department of Indian Affairs on membership questions?

The minister of Indian Affairs, Mr Munro, has indicated that he will lift the effect of section 12(1)b and section 12(4) for any band that so requests (using a power given by section 4[2] of the Indian Act). It appears that Mr Munro has agreed to do this against advice given by the Department of Justice. What he is doing is taking two elements out of a larger membership system. The removal of section 12(1)b will, inevitably, give rise to future problems in the administration of the membership system.

I assume that Mr Munro is willing to create problems in the administration of membership in order to force the process of legislative change. If substantial problems arise, the federal case for changing the legislation is strengthened. It will be strengthened in favour of the federal government's proposals for retaining central authority over membership but removing the sexual discrimination from the present system. Alternatively, if the bands create the problem in the administration of membership by taking control themselves, they will force change in their favour. The easiest resolution of the problem caused by band non-compliance will be a system of assigning jurisdiction over membership to the bands themselves.

We have a history of band innovation or assumption of control in certain areas. The clearest areas are in relation to the internal landholding system on reserves, residency rights of non-members on reserves, and voting rights in band-council elections. It may be that we can anticipate some band innovation in terms of membership in the years immediately ahead. The by-law passed by the Spallumcheen band is clearly an innovation and may prove successful. The general unwillingness of the bands to assume jurisdiction has had the effect of leaving the initiative for change largely in the hands of the Department of Indian Affairs and of Parliament. If Indian government is to be achieved in any meaningful sense, this passivity on the part of bands must end.

Notes

1 *Natural Parents* v *Superintendent of Child Welfare* (1975) 60 DLR (3d) 148
2 *Regina* v *Gingrich* (1958) 29 WWR 471
3 *Regina* v *Sacobie* (1980) 30 NBR (2d) 70
4 *Cardinal* v *Attorney-General of Alberta* (1974) SCR 695
5 *Four B* v *United Garment Workers* (1979) 102 DLR (3d) 385
6 *Western Industrial* v *Scarcee Developments* (1979) 98 DLR (3d) 424
7 See n 6.
8 The case was argued before the Alberta Court of Appeal in February 1981.

J. RICK PONTING / ROGER GIBBINS

Thorns in the Bed of Roses: A Socio-political View of the Problems of Indian Government

Introduction

To write on the problems of Indian government is a risky venture for at least two reasons. First, it invites the ancient response whereby the bearer of bad news was himself subjected to attack. Second, at the time of writing Indian government is still only loosely defined and likely to be highly variable in form.

With regard to the first of these points we wish to stress that in identifying the pitfalls of Indian government we are not taking a position on the desirability of Indian government. We are merely pointing out problems of which the architects of Indian government will have to be cognizant. It is for the Indian people, not non-Indian academics like ourselves, to weigh the advantages and problems of Indian government and decide on its acceptability. With regard to the second point, we have dealt with the amorphousness of Indian government by treating Indian government somewhat as a 'black box.' That is, rather than addressing the specifics of one or another model of Indian government, we have instead treated Indian government as a relatively abstract concept. The assumptions we make about the nature of Indian government are of a highly general, non-contentious nature and include the following:

1 Indian government will have a territorial base on the reserves, although its reach may not be restricted to that base.
2 Indian government will involve some form of administrative and political amalgamation at the supra-band level (tribal, district, or national).

3 Indian government will entail the transfer of certain jurisdictional responsibilities now in the hands of the federal government to Indian hands.
4 Indian decisions with respect to these responsibilities will not be subject to
review or veto by the federal government.
5 Indian governments will have access to and control over sufficient fiscal
resources to meet these responsibilities.

Although some of these assumptions may not be appropriate for some
forms of Indian government, they are generally applicable.

Advantages of Indian Government

Although we will concentrate our attention on the problems of Indian
government, some of the important advantages of Indian government
should be briefly acknowledged before we proceed. While Indian government is not a panacea, it is an institutional innovation that may
attenuate, although not eliminate, several sociological problems facing
Indians in Canada today.

One such problem is the racism that exists in certain sectors of the
larger Canadian society. Here the literature relating equal-status intergroup contact with reduction in prejudice and discrimination, while not
at all definitive, would suggest that the conferring of governmental status on Indian organizations would enhance the perceptions of Indians
held by the general Canadian public. Beyond this direct impact we
would argue that the changes in Indian behaviours (for example, a
decrease in skid-row alcoholism) that, over the long run, Indian government can reasonably be expected to bring will lead to further changes
in those perceptions and in the behaviour towards Indians that they
engender.

Elsewhere[1] we have described the Indian and Inuit Affairs Programme
(IIAP) of the Department of Indian Affairs and Northern Development
(DIAND) as an organization that seeks to exercise social control over
Indians. Here one of the compelling attractions of Indian government is
that it would end the blatant paternalism and external control of IIAP
and DIAND, including manipulative governmental control based on the
power of the purse strings, or what we have labelled elsewhere 'socio-
fiscal' control.[2] Rather than Indian organizations being accountable to

non-Indian government bureaucrats for federal funds received, block grants could be made to Indian governments. Indian organizations and bureaucrats could then be held responsible to elected Indian governments just as provincial bureaucrats who receive federal block grants are responsible to the elected members of the provincial government. One cloud on the horizon, however, is that even in its dealings with provincial governments Ottawa seems to be moving away from block funding and back to a system of conditional grants-in-aid where it largely sets the conditions. Thus the advent of Indian government could be expected to weaken but not eliminate socio-fiscal control.

While the 'social-disorganization' and 'anomie' school of thought on social problems has met with deserved criticism in the sociological literature,[3] the fact remains that some Indian communities – probably a smaller number than is usually assumed by non-Indian observers – do exhibit many signs of social disorganization and anomie. Indian government can realistically be expected to ameliorate such social disorganization and anomie, especially in so far as it involves explicit attempts at 'nation-building.' Here we refer to the development of social solidarity, of shared collective goals, and of an institutional and economic base that will enable the Indian community to exercise a much greater degree of self-determination. The nation-building efforts of Indian governments will enhance Indians' cultural pride, provide successful role models, and generate a more positive self-image on the part of Indians who observe the accomplishments of their 'all-Indian' governments. Attended by such accomplishments and, indeed, almost by virtue of taking the decision to create Indian government, social disorganization and anomie will be dealt a severe blow.

A final advantage of Indian government that we wish to cite here is its potential contribution to 'boundary maintenance.' The concept of boundary maintenance refers to the making and keeping of distinctions between groups and to the retention of barriers to social interaction between groups. Indians have long faced severe problems of boundary maintenance as they have been subjected to forced acculturation (for example, in the residential schools) and deculturation (for example, the banning of certain social and religious ceremonies). Indians have adopted non-Indian religions, ceded (or had stolen) Indian lands, intermarried with non-Indians, moved off the reserves into predominantly non-Indian urban areas, entered the non-Indian industrial system, and even

had Indian children removed from Indian families and placed in adop-
tive non-Indian homes. With Indian government in place, Indians could
more effectively resist or reverse many of those phenomena or at least
play a role in setting the terms and conditions under which those phenomena will occur. Indeed, to fail to do so would be almost suicidal for
Indian government as an institution.

Thus, Indian government has many attractive features and consequences, not all of which have been discussed above. However, it is not
without its drawbacks, problems, and limitations. Even a bed of roses has
its thorns, and it is to the thorny issues of Indian government that we
now turn. We shall consider two broad sets of problems, those internal to
the Indian community and those that are to be found in the relationship
between Indians and the larger non-Indian society. While some of the
problems arise from Indian government itself, others are existing problems that either are not alleviated by the creation of Indian governments
or may actually be exacerbated by the creation of Indian governments.

Problems Internal to the Indian Community

Rising Expectations

Politicians being what they are, the attainment of Indian government is
likely to be accompanied by lavish rhetorical promises of its benefits,
potential, and comparative advantages over the former colonial regime.
Accompanying this is likely to be a multiplicity of demands, something
faced by governments everywhere these days but likely to be particularly
acute for Indian governments in light of the numerous and severe problems Indians face. Unless Indians are far more cynical than we realize,
the probable outcome is that Indians will come to hold very high expectations of their Indian governments. These expectations, however, may
prove to be unrealistic in light of such facts as severe shortages in the
skilled Indian labour force that would be needed to staff the Indian civil
service, Indians' lack of experience at policy formulation, and Indians'
lack of experience at designing and implementing programs to carry out
policy decisions.[4] The achievements of Indian government will also be
severely constrained by very high per capita overhead costs in the
delivery of services due to an inability to take advantage of economies of
scale. This will be particularly true if the unit of Indian political organi-

zation encompasses Indian communities that are widely dispersed geographically. If rising expectations meet more with frustration than with fulfilment, cynicism and apathy could mount, and the cause of Indian development would be dealt a heavy blow from which it would not soon recover.

Intensification of Social Tensions

While Indians and non-Indians alike argue in favour of Indians assuming more responsibility for their own affairs, it is sometimes overlooked that inherent in the concept of responsibility is the acceptance of blame when things go wrong. Indian government will mean the loss of DIAND-IIAP as a scapegoat or whipping boy; when things go wrong, as they inevitably do, Indian politicians will have to shoulder the blame. As a consequence, existing political cleavages within Indian communities may be deepened and new ones may open.

If Indian government is organized at a national or regional level, we can expect historical tribal rivalries to be brought into bold relief, particularly when the stakes will be higher than perhaps ever before and Indian politicians are shouldering full responsibility. If, instead, Indian government is strictly a local phenomenon, we can similarly expect that existing cleavages between social classes[5] and clans will be accentuated. Indeed, our suspicion is that both contemporary Indian nationalism and the Indian government it seeks to achieve will benefit the Indian middle class much more than the Indian lower class, just as the nationalism of Quebec's Quiet Revolution benefited the Québécois middle class much more than the Québécois working class. Given that Quebec has undergone marked class polarization since the Quiet Revolution,[6] it is at least conceivable that the same could be in store for Indians.

Another factor to be taken into consideration with regard to internal cleavages is the need for developing allocative mechanisms to redistribute wealth among Indian communities, if not among individual Indians. If Indian government exists at a supra-band level, and so long as marked economic disparities among bands persist, there will be a need for Indian government to act as a vehicle for the redistribution of wealth. Attaining consensus on the mechanisms of redistribution will be by no means an easy task, as can be seen from the contemporary dispute between the Alberta and Ontario provincial governments over the

Alberta Heritage Savings Trust Fund and from the dispute between the federal and Alberta governments over the resource-taxation and energy-pricing provisions of the 1980 federal budget. If it were to exist at the national level, where there are over five hundred and seventy bands, Indian government would face an enormously more complex redistribution problem than that faced by the Canadian federal government in dealing with a mere ten provinces among whom the differences in wealth are far less than among Indian bands. Thus, the prospects for increased tensions among bands are very real under Indian government.

Rights and Duties of Off-Reserve Indians

Under Indian government, tensions may also mount between reserve and off-reserve Indians over the issue of the rights and duties of the latter. Here again the Quebec case is instructive. In the evolution of Québécois nationalism the Quebec government, responding to the strategic opportunities and constraints in its environment, gradually abandoned the pursuit of special rights and powers for Francophones outside its territorial borders. Just as Quebec has essentially 'given up' on Francophones living outside Quebec, Indian governments may come to 'give up' on Indians living off-reserve. It should be noted, however, that the loss for Indian governments would be greater than for Quebec; not only does a higher proportion of the Indian population live off-reserve than does the Canadian Francophone population live outside Quebec, but the inducements for Indians to live off-reserve probably exceed the inducements for Francophones to leave Quebec.

Indian government may thus become a two-edged sword. Indians may find that, rather than enjoying the benefits of participating in both an Indian-governed sphere and the larger society, they have to make a choice between the two. To the extent that straddling or 'commuting' between the Indian and non-Indian worlds has been a successful mode of adaptation for many Indians, to have that mobility precluded or more severely restricted would be an unfortunate cost of Indian government. Excessively rigid boundary maintenance could force many to leave the group. Conversely, pronounced differentials in the rights and privileges of on-reserve and off-reserve Indians, which Indian government will produce, might not only foster resentment on the part of the off-reserve Indians but could also increase the population pressure on reserve lands and facilities by effectively removing the safety valve of off-reserve migration.

Demand Aggregation and Consensus Building

From the perspective of geography, ethnicity, culture, and politics, Canada can be seen as a highly artificial entity. Ours is not a homogeneous society held together in a relatively compact space by commonalities of origin, culture, or ideology. Canada has been imposed and superimposed upon the North American aboriginal peoples who themselves are markedly heterogeneous. We thus have a situation in which one artificial entity (Canada) creates other artificial entities (Indian bands encompassing rival clans, status–non-status distinctions, provincial associations that encompass long-standing rivalries, administrative districts, and so on). As a result the task of aggregating Indian demands and moulding them into a durable consensus has become truly Herculean.

Indians have responded to this situation with eloquent rhetoric, with forceful articulation of what they do not want, and with a brand of politics that emphasizes the positional[7] and symbolic aspects of their relationship with the non-Indian government. However, with the advent of Indian government the positional and symbolic victories will, by definition, have been won, and symbolic and oppositional politics will no longer suffice. Indian governments will have to articulate and aggregate the demands of their diverse constituents, formulate policies, build political support for those policies, and then implement effective programs that will meet the needs of different Indian communities. In short, Indian governments will have to deliver the goods, and in trying to do so may find traditional methods of consensus decision-making incapable of serving a very heterogeneous and conflictual electorate.

At various points in this paper we have identified factors that militate against success in delivering the goods. Our concern is that Indian governments that cannot surmount the kinds of problems discussed may experience a loss of legitimacy in the Indian community and a subsequent loss of commitment by members of that community. Such an eventuality would knock two very crucial pillars out from under Indian government. However, we are not suggesting that potential failure should deter Indians from creating Indian governments. Rather we are pointing to the need for sound advice, for planning, and for communicative mechanisms that would enable Indian governments to learn from the problems, successes, and failures of each other.

Problems in the Indian–Non-Indian Relationship

As noted earlier, there are problems in the relations between Indians and the larger society that either are not addressed by the creation of Indian governments or may actually be exacerbated by the creation of Indian governments. It is to several of these we now turn.

Problems of Economic Structure

The Canadian economy is a capitalistic one that is dominated by multi-national corporations – many of which are foreign-owned – and organized in a 'hinterland-metropolis' structure that stretches beyond the borders of Canada itself. These basic economic features are beyond the power of Indian governments to change. Although at times they may present attractive opportunities for Indian governments (for example, investment in energy-development projects on the 'frontier'), they none the less constitute powerful forces that are capable of buffeting national governments much more powerful than any Indian government can ever hope to be. The relationships between the government of Canada and the Massey-Harris and Chrysler corporations provide cases in point.

The driving force in capitalism is profit maximization through growth. To achieve this goal, corporations create new wants and 'needs' in the populace through advertising, which in turn makes possible the modern media of mass communication through which the citizens of Indian government will be bombarded daily with messages promoting non-Indian lifestyles, values, consumer goods, and services. This bombardment cannot help but shape Indian aspirations (pro or con) and, in the process, generate demands on Indian government to facilitate the attainment of the desirable and to protect Indian communities from the impact of the undesirable. Such demands, which will not be easily met, illustrate the types of problems that Indian governments will face, problems over and above the political ones that have preoccupied Indian organizations for the last decade.

The fact that the Canadian economy is dominated by multinational corporations also has important implications for Indian governments seeking economic development for their people. While such corporations do not have the power to undertake development entirely on their own terms, as the Mackenzie Valley pipeline issue of 1977 illustrated, their power is very considerable indeed. They have the money and skilled personnel to generate massive volumes of technical data on their behalf, and they have the money to hire the very best lawyers to argue their cases before the highest courts in the land. They are capable of offering substantial inducements to co-opt Indian leaders or skilled Indian technicians or otherwise to get their own way through the offering of jobs, grants, and electoral-campaign contributions. In addition they usually are fully capable of going elsewhere if they do not get their own way or if the comparative advantages of one location over another change. Thus, while Indian government may provide an instrument through which Indian communities can bargain with multinational corporations, it does not provide an instrument of control.

Finally, with regard to matters of economic structure, we have the condition that Canada is organized on a 'hinterland-metropolis' basis such that the development of some regions is actively promoted at the expense of other regions, which are deliberately kept in a state of underdevelopment. This raises questions concerning the extent to which new Indian centres of economic power will be allowed to develop in competition with the established centres of economic power in the metropolis. If and when head-to-head competition occurs between a 'crown corporation' of Indian government and a subsidiary of an established conglomerate from the metropolis, the deck is stacked in favour of the latter and the continued existence of the former may be threatened.

Intergovernmental Relations

The abolition or emasculation of DIAND-IIAP as a consequence of Indian government will create in turn new problems in intergovernmental relations. Indian government will itself be staffed by bureaucrats – Indian bureaucrats, perhaps, but bureaucrats nevertheless. Indeed, the case of Harold Cardinal's term as the most senior IIAP bureaucrat in Alberta demonstrates that in dealing with an Indian clientele, Indian bureaucrats sometimes face handicaps and vulnerabilities that non-Indians do not.[8] Furthermore, allegations that Ottawa withheld federal funds in order to

punish the Newfoundland government for its 'intransigence' on constitutional matters[9] would suggest, if true, that Indian governments may
still have to endure blatant socio-fiscal control at the hands of the federal
government.

Relations between Indian governments and the federal and provincial
governments will not be conducted solely on the bureaucratic plane.
More likely is a situation of 'executive federalism,'[10] wherein bargaining
will take place among the political executives (cabinet ministers, first
ministers, and senior civil servants) of the various governments. Several
implications of this merit mention. Indian governments are unlikely to
enjoy exclusive jurisdiction in any functional realm; the direction and
shape of policy on many matters will likely have to be worked out in a
continual process of bargaining, compromise, negotiation, and consultation with the federal and/or provincial governments. As this is the norm
in contemporary federal-provincial relations, it will likely hold true for
Indian governments as well. Here it should also be noted that the federal-provincial intergovernmental process depends upon the various
participants being able to commit their governments without being concerned about ratification in the House of Commons or provincial legislative assemblies, since ratification of executive agreements is all but a
formality. If Indian governments were to join this intergovernmental
process, they too would have to be able to negotiate on behalf of their
constituents without having to worry about subsequent ratification from
individual bands, tribal associations, or provincial organizations. Thus,
the price of admission to executive federalism and effective participation in the intergovernmental process will be a substantial loss of local
autonomy.

A particularly thorny issue will be that of determining which parts of
which federal and provincial laws and regulations will and will not
apply on Indian reserves. Problems such as the applicability of provincial
game laws will not disappear with the creation of Indian governments.
Moreover, during periods of competition and expansion between federal
and provincial governments, Indian governments (especially in Alberta
and Quebec) may be caught in the midst of conflicting federal and
provincial claims, just as oil companies have been during the dispute
between the governments of Newfoundland and Canada over the issue
of ownership of offshore resources. If Indian governments join in the

fray, Indian individuals may get caught in the midst of a three-way intergovernmental power struggle in which their own government is one of the contending parties.

Several other problems related to executive federalism and jurisdictional domains also arise. First, there is the possibility that Indian governments will be outnegotiated by federal and provincial governments, which have a larger pool of technical and negotiating expertise upon which they will be able to draw.[11] In casting off the constraining aspects of federal government paternalism, Indian governments will also give up many of the protective features of that paternalism and can accordingly expect to suffer some costly losses in the intergovernmental gladiatorial ring. Second, Indian governments may prove to be particularly vulnerable to the federal government's practice of committing other governments to expensive shared-cost programs from which the federal government subsequently and suddenly withdraws its financial participation.

Third, the question arises whether Indians will have access to federal and provincial services (for example, higher education and social assistance) provided to non-Indians. Will Indian governments themselves deny Indians access to certain such services, and, if not, will the federal or provincial governments deny that access? Access may be dependent upon the payment of provincial and federal taxes, and thus Indians may be required to support their own Indian governments along with the federal and provincial governments already in place. Alternatively, Indians could be denied federal and provincial services, in which case a full range of equivalent services would have to be provided by Indian governments. The cost of doing so at equivalent levels of quality could be staggering given the small size and dispersed location of the Indian population. With the interests of empire-building government bureaucrats – both Indian and non-Indian – being threatened regardless of which way this issue is broached, it could become a contentious issue in the executive-federalism forum.

Indian Sovereignty and the Federal Government

There remains the question and problem of how Indians will fit into the national political community, or the status of Indians as Canadian and provincial citizens should Indian governments be created. In Western liberal democracies such as Canada, persons are usually incorporated into the polity on an individualistic basis. All persons have equal rights in law as individuals, and their membership in one or another racial or political group is irrelevant to their voting rights, civil rights, and eligibility to receive government benefits, services, and protections. Group rights per se do not exist. For example, French Canadians do not have special linguistic rights in Canada; rather, every Canadian has the right to practise the official language of his or her choice. The very concept of special rights for one or another racial or political group is abhorrent to the small-l liberal ideology, notwithstanding the Trudeau government's affirmation of aboriginal rights in its constitutional Charter of Human Rights in 1981.[12]

Indians, however, bring a different value system to the Canadian polity. The Indian value system stresses co-operation, a collectivity orientation, and special rights for Indians as a group. Indians are aware of the inconsistency between the liberal ideology of individual equality on the one hand and the provision of special rights (for example, language and education rights) to the two so-called 'founding peoples' on the other. Indians seek at least coequal status, as a group, with the two 'founding peoples' and implementation of the group rights that will preserve that status.

Indian government is one expression of such group rights, one that, because of its inconsistency with the liberal ideology, will likely meet with resistance from the larger non-Indian society. Canadians have already demonstrated during the 1980 Quebec referendum campaign that they have little sympathy with notions of divided sovereignty, and sovereignty over Indians will not be easily ceded to Indians by other Canadians. This problem might be attenuated if Indian governments become like provinces and thus abandon any claim to sovereignty per se, but it is not clear whether this sacrifice of sovereignty would be acceptable to Indian politicians. Even if it were, Indian government may still be seen by non-Indians as a violation of the basic tenets of the liberal ideology whereby persons are incorporated into the polity as individuals rather than as members of groups.

In concluding we must raise a potential problem relating to Indians' participation in the Canadian federal government. If Indians acquire a unique governmental structure, what position would they then have in the House of Commons? Would their federal representatives be seated in a separate chamber or merely in an embassy entirely outside the Houses of Parliament? If seated in the House of Commons, would Indians be integrated into the existing party system and thereby have the opportunity of winning representation in the national government, or would they form an isolated faction with little influence? If the latter, would the New Democratic Party tolerate such a threat to its position of holding the balance of power during minority governments such as that of 1972–4? In short, under Indian government will Indians have even less influence over federal-level decisions affecting them (for example, oil taxation) than they do now? The price of local autonomy may well be an even more weakened voice at the centre.

Notes

1 J. Rick Ponting and Roger Gibbins *Out of Irrelevance: A Socio-political Introduction to Indian Affairs in Canada* (Scarborough, Ont: Butterworths 1980) 103–4
2 Ibid, 124–5
3 See, for example, Richard Henshel and Anne Marie Henshel *Perspectives on Social Problems* (Don Mills, Ont: Longmans 1973) 42–5.
4 Indeed, it has only been within the last five years or less that some national Indian leaders have overcome a reaction of fear and intimidation to that mystical word 'policy.'
5 Edgar Dosman *Indians: The Urban Dilemma* (Toronto: McClelland & Stewart 1972) 56–7
6 Kenneth McRoberts and Dale Posgate *Quebec: Social Change and Political Crisis* (Toronto: McClelland & Stewart 1973) 142–4
7 Sally M. Weaver *Making Indian Policy in Canada: The Hidden Agenda 1968–70* (Toronto: University of Toronto Press 1981)
8 See Ponting and Gibbins *Out of Irrelevance* 147–51.
9 Reported in 'Punishment for Criticism – Ottawa Cuts Funds: MP' *Calgary Herald* 8 January 1981
10 Donald Smiley *Canada in Question: Federalism in the Seventies* 2nd edn (Toronto: McGraw-Hill Ryerson 1976); Ponting and Gibbins *Out of Irrelevance* 319–20
11 For instance, in parallel fashion it is said that prior to the creation of Petro-Canada and the injection of its expertise into the federal camp, the federal government was sometimes outnegotiated by virtue of the

sheer superiority of the expertise on the negotiating teams of the oil companies and the oil-producing provinces.

12 All-party agreement to a constitutional clause recognizing and affirming aboriginal rights was, to say the least, not easily attained. This clause, contradicting a basic tenet of the liberal ideology, was resisted for years by the government of the day. Although its attainment was an occasion for rejoicing in some Indian and other native circles, it must be stressed that the struggle is far from over. It will continue as competing interpretations and limits are placed on the rather vague clause and as policies and agreements issuing therefrom are transformed in the stage of implementation.

5 Social, Economic, and Organizational Requisites for Indian Government

IF INDIAN GOVERNMENT is to be realized, a number of organizational, political, social, and economic conditions must be fulfilled. The papers in this part provide a diverse native perspective on the requisites for Indian self-government. Several common threads run through the presentations. First, all of the Indian leaders argue that native peoples must re-establish their traditional institutions and reassert their traditional political and cultural values. Indian culture and spirituality are held to be critically 'unique' requirements of self-determination. Second, as a strategy for achieving self-government all of the writers advocate control of those institutions that impact on them most directly. And third, they hold that Indians must establish financial independence from the federal government. Only through economic independence can any degree of political autonomy be obtained.

In the first essay, Andrew Delisle discusses how his people, the Mohawks, have taken steps towards acquiring control over health care, policing, and other services on his reserve. He argues that Indians must be innovative and assertive in their interpretation of the Indian Act if they want to progress down the road of self-determination. In the second paper, Earl Old Person, chief of the Blackfoot nation in Montana, describes how American Indians have attempted to break out of the political, economic, and legal constraints established by the United States government. He focuses on the development of tribal enterprises, such as the successful Blackfoot pencil factory, as examples of how Indians can begin to achieve economic self-sufficiency. Next, Sol Sanderson describes how the Federation of Saskatchewan Indians is establishing the organizational structures to exercise its jurisdictional authority in Sas-

katchewan. At the same time they are working to strengthen the internal
authority of bands by reasserting traditional institutions such as the
chieftainship. The last two selections, by Del Riley and Sykes Powerface,
provide significant insights into the difficulties that Indian leadership
faces in the drive for self-government. For them, Indian political organizations must break the bonds of financial dependence on the federal government if they are to be effective in their negotiations with federal and
provincial officials. However, they argue, these efforts must be accompanied by the willingness of Indians across Canada to come together
behind their provincial and federal organizations to enable them to exercise strong leadership. These two contributions underscore the difficulties
that such a culturally diverse group as native Indians are experiencing in
achieving a united political front vis-à-vis the federal government.

ANDREW DELISLE

How We Regained Control over Our Lives and Territories: The Kahnawake Story

Much confusion has arisen of late over the use of terms such as 'sovereignty,' 'nation,' and 'Indian government.' It is my belief that non-Indians do not understand what we Indians are talking about when we use these terms because they have their own definition of sovereignty, nation, and Indian government. I will deal here with Indian government. There is no alternative to total Indian self-government. The federal government tells us that our spiritual values have no place in politics, but if we are going to build a truly Indian society, spirituality must be involved in everything we do, including our government. What do we mean by Indian government? How do we go about governing ourselves?

I will start off by telling you a brief history of myself. I was raised in Kahnawake. I was born there and educated there. My father was an elected chief. My grandfather also was an elected chief. When I grew up I saw a lot of things happen. My father dealt in coal. When I was young I went with my father across the Mercier Bridge, which was about five miles from my reserve, to buy twenty bags of coal. He would sell them for a twenty-five-cent profit, so that we would exist. On many occasions I saw him, as the chief, answer the door to Indian people who had asked the Indian agents for assistance to heat their house and had been refused. They were freezing and my father told them to go ahead and take a bag of coal off that pile. They didn't have to pay for it.

My father was not able to read. Once I saw my father sitting in front of a meeting and the government official gave him the paper upside-down, and then laughed at him. I saw these things and I remember them. But I always felt that there is good in every man and that I should attempt my best to try to find that good, so that my people could benefit from what these non-Indian people knew. For all of the twenty-odd years that I have been in Indian politics, I have watched and I have tried in every area to improve the condition of my people.

My generation has experienced many profound changes. It was during my generation that the law was rescinded so that now we can become educated and not lose our status as an Indian. It was in my generation that the law was rescinded so that Indians were recognized as being Canadian. It was only in 1965 that the Quebec government gave me at least a semblance of equality by offering me the right to vote, which of course I did not accept. Those things all happened in my generation. I tell you these things because it is not only myself but Indian people across the country who remember and think of these things. That is why we are now so impatient and aggressive in seeking change.

All during the time that I was growing up, my mother, my father, and my grandfather said that it is not good to have a stranger running our affairs. Although they didn't adhere strictly to the traditional Iroquoian system, my mother, father, and grandfather always thought of it and used its philosophy as an ideal. This is why I have continued to learn more and more about it, and a few years ago I came to the firm realization that there was no other alternative for our people but to go back to that traditional system, which enabled my people to survive for generations in spite of the bad things that had been done to them. They survived in spite of the abrogation of treaties by the Canadian government, in spite of the false offers of goodwill that had been presented to them, in spite of the oppression they have lived under, and in spite of being cut off from an educational system that would have enabled them to learn the ways of the non-Indians so that they could share in their knowledge. In spite of all this the Iroquoian people survived. It must have been for a reason. The other Indian nations across the country also survived and, I suspect, for basically the same reason – because they possess something that cannot be destroyed.

In the beginning we were a scattered people; then we formed bands. The bands formed tribes; the tribes formed nations; the nations formed confederacies. Then the white man came and divided our nations. They were broken down by design, from nations to tribes to bands and, in some cases, to settlements. Isn't that what we are facing now? But there is a great circle, and that circle repeats itself. Our objective is to put everything back together as it was before the white man came, to ensure that the circle continues.

We talk about Indian government, and we try to come up with the best structures. I don't have to find a new structure. We already have a ready-made structure – the traditional structure of Indian government. When we attempted to re-establish our self-government and our sovereignty through negotiations with the federal government, first in regard to the Indian Act and then the Constitution, they laughed at us. They said, 'Ha, you'll never get together. Ha, what you're asking for is stupid. Ha, you know this is one country, not six as the Six Nations of the Iroquois think.' But today the federal government is having its own problems with Quebec and Newfoundland and the West. All the things they laughed at us for are happening to them. That circle has come full around as it always does when people don't watch out what they are doing. But the circle is not understood by the non-Indian.

What is the current situation on the reserves (actually, I prefer to call them territories)? Right now in my territory, if I strictly followed the Indian Act, as I have been told by the Indian Affairs Branch that I must do, I would not be able to educate my children. I would not have any justice for my people. I would not be an administrator for the benefit of Indian people but only an administrator for the benefit of Indian Affairs. So, to serve the best interests of my people, I have to do things which are out-of-the-ordinary. If there is going to be any improvement in our condition, we have to do things that are out-of-the-ordinary, at least that are not ordinary in the minds of the politicians and the Indian Affairs Branch bureaucrats. Our people, who base their thinking on natural law, think it is ordinary, but to people who don't respect natural law, we are out-of-the-ordinary.

Right now Indian people are sitting on the fence, damning the Indian Act but afraid to abolish it. Our people are reluctant to change the Indian Act for fear that the purse-strings of the federal government are going to be tightened or treaty and aboriginal rights will be abrogated. But if we keep sitting on the fence, I think past experience tells us which side we're going to fall on. So we have to make a move, and I advocate the traditional way – in my case, the Iroquoian way. My objective is to get those of my people that have strayed away from our traditions, like I myself once did, to understand and come back. It's not easy. I suspect this is the problem with Indian people everywhere. We have to sit down with each other within our own communities. We have to reconcile the factions that exist. We have to tell those people who just want money or glory for themselves that they must think of the nation first. We have to sit down and speak the truth to each other, and make a great peace amongst each other. That peace will bring unity and with unity there is strength, and with strength we can start assuming control over our own affairs.

I will use my territory as an example of what can be done to start assuming control over our own affairs. First, my people took over control of their own health services from the Indian Affairs Branch. Everybody said it was illegal. 'You can't do it,' they said; 'You don't have any money.' But we took over our hospital and our clinics in 1961 and 1966, and now we have a forty-two-bed hospital operating fully without government assistance. I don't mean to brag when I say that. My intention is to stress the positive, to say that it can be done. Sure, we subscribe to the provincial medicare program, because we feel it is our right to benefit from the development of the natural resources within our province and we do it primarily to maintain the health of our people. Importantly, however, we provide the services our way, and we work towards our own objectives.

Second, we took over the police services. There was always a fight as to who controlled policing on our reserve – whether it was the federal government, the provincial government, or us. One day our council gave a direction to our police and they refused to carry it out because, they said, it was illegal according to the Indian Act and Criminal Code. However, we believed it was right for our people and our people believed it was right for them, so we dismissed the police force. We replaced them with 'peacekeepers.' I should say that even a peacekeeper force is not entirely consistent with our traditional philosophy. Traditionally, we did not need anyone to watch over us because we believed in not doing wrong to each other or committing a bad act. However, we have not yet gone fully back to our traditional ways. But at least peacekeepers are a bit more in line with our traditional values. The provincial and federal governments don't recognize our peacekeepers. They consider them to be illegal. The federal government provides us with subsidies for training 'law-enforcement officers' because they say they do not recognize peacekeepers. We accept the subsidies because the money belongs to us. We do not consider it as a hand-out from the government. Unfortunately, we have to kiss somebody's butt to get it, and that is a thorn in our side, but it's our money and we need it. Until we find a way to get it without kissing someone's butt, we will have to keep on doing it.

A third thing that we've done, again on the basis of our own Indian legislation, is to send our children to English-language schools. The provincial government tried to force us to ask permission to go to an Eng-lish-language school. We said, 'Iroquois people, especially Mohawks, don't ask for any permission to talk any language, so we are not asking.' They said, 'Well, you can't go to any of our schools,' and we said, 'Okay, we are going to put schools in our own reserves.' They said, 'Oh, you can't do that. The high schools, colleges, and universities won't recognize your children's education.' But we went ahead and did it, and we negoti-ated on our own and got our schools recognized. They still say that everything we are doing is illegal, but it's not jeopardizing any other city or town around my place, my territory. It's benefiting my people, so how can it be wrong? Can it be wrong just because the law says that we as 'little Indians' can't do anything unless the government allows us to do it? So you see, you have to take some things into your own hands and you have to do them now.

In our territory the Canadian government has introduced land allot-ment. That is an individual Certificate of Possession system, and the government is now attempting to push it a little bit further so that indi-viduals will be allowed to sell individual plots of land. Federal officials use these tricks to get us fighting among ourselves, and we must stop them from doing this to us. Because of that outside interference our people spend much time arguing with each other, and while we are attacking each other over some government program or policy, the gov-ernment takes the land out from under our feet. This is what we have to stop.

We should be more willing and prepared to help each other. I am not ashamed to say we need other Iroquois people to help us, and if not other Iroquois, then other native people. Let us take, for example, the peace-keepers that I mentioned earlier. We have ten men, and those ten men, as far as we are concerned, are there not only to enforce band by-laws but to protect our lands against trespassers from outside. If we are opposed to highway development or a dam project or anything like that, those men will be in the front line defending us. But what if we run into a confrontation that is bigger than we can handle? When we need more help, I should be able to call on my native brothers and say I need some assistance, and they should be willing to come over. This is something that existed naturally in the past. You didn't have to make any special arrangements. It was generally recognized that if one group was in trouble, the other would come running to help out. This need of assis-tance may surface in our territory tomorrow, the next day, or the day after. The government of Quebec is talking about building a dam on my reserve, not only one but two, and my people have said, 'We'll be damned if you are going to build that dam in our territory.' We may need your help when the show-down comes.

Another area where we could help each other is through intertribal trade. Some of the best moccasins you can find anywhere are manufactured on the Peigan Reserve. The best denims and pencils are made by Blackfoot Indians in Montana. There is beautiful leather work being done on the Blood Reserve, so on and on. There is hardly an Indian community in Canada that cannot put its hand to some kind of useful work and turn out better-quality products than you can get elsewhere. Why don't we all, as Indian people, support each other with such enterprises? Then you will see how fast we can make it. You would be surprised to see how fast some of these Indian communities which now survive on welfare cheques could become financially self-supporting and independent if we co-operated with each other and bought goods from each other. This is what we can do tomorrow if we just put our minds to it. Even though we are a geographically scattered people, we can still assist each other. Rather than viewing the distance between ourselves as a handicap, we should study ways of taking advantage of the fact that we are scattered.

I think we can apply this kind of positive approach to a number of areas of concern. For instance, a lot of Indians are afraid of getting rid of the Indian Act. Well, we are not advocating getting rid of it; we are just telling our people to take advantage of this legislation. We must treat it as *enabling* legislation to allow us to implement those things that have been granted us in the treaties. It is true that the government over the years has interpreted this legislation to its own advantage, banking on what they view as our stupidity. You have heard them say it: 'Those guys don't know anything – they don't know how to count money, they don't know how to keep records, they don't know who is an Indian and who isn't,' and so on. So they kept the records, and then they said, 'Well, since those guys don't know anything, I guess we will have to tell them how it is,' and they proceeded to do it. We were not stupid, but we did misplace our confidence by trusting them. We believed people wouldn't cheat and lie to other people. Suddenly we woke up and we found out the truth.

I have tried to sit down and work with government officials, but their objective always is assimilation, disintegration, and annihilation of Indian peoples. Their goal is to get rid of us. But we won't give up. We have a place, not only on this continent but in the world, and we have something to offer. Those same people who tried to take away our identity are now looking for an identity of their own. I don't have to look for an identity – I know I'm Mohawk. You know you're Blackfoot; you know you're Cree. Do they know what a Canadian is? Ask one of those people sitting in Parliament what a Canadian is. You will get as many different interpretations as there are members of Parliament. I feel sorry for them.

I know that we can control our own affairs and our destiny starting today. I for one would support the abolition of the Indian Affairs Department right now and replace it with an Indian-run bureaucratic structure. The civil servants will say, 'Why, you're creating a brown bureaucracy.' They don't say that because they are interested in our welfare; they just don't want to lose their jobs, that's all. Why do we hesitate to take over the administration of education and justice in our territories? We need to take over the education of our children because we want them educated the way our grandfathers ordained they should be. We want to take over the justice system because we want to have what we consider true justice. We are not satisfied to let other people run our systems of education and justice. The development and control of our educational system can be done tomorrow if we really want to. The application of laws for our own benefit instead of for the benefit of the government can be done tomorrow if we really want to.

Unfortunately, some of our people don't understand what we are trying to accomplish by changing to Indian government. The disturbing thing is that they judge change on the basis of whether it benefits them personally, not the community. The attitude is, 'I'm for it when it helps me, but I'm against it when it doesn't help me.' We cannot continue to hold such an attitude. We must stand for the common good of our people, whether Mohawk or Cree or Blackfoot or whatever. And if we compromise on this, we are going to lose. We have compromised in the past, and we have lost in the past. This is something that we all have to understand. We must strive to achieve that situation where we will be truthful with each other, peaceful with each other, unified with each other. This in turn will bring strength, and that strength will make us supreme.

CHIEF EARL OLD PERSON

Problems, Prospects, and Aspirations of the 'Real People' in America

Our elders are the backbone of the Indian nations. Today, they look to the young Indian leaders for the continuing survival of our people, for maintaining and preserving our culture and our lands. I don't refer to our lands as 'reservations' or 'reserves' because I don't feel these lands were reserved by the American government for us. These lands were protected for us by our forefathers. Those brave and strong men fought and died for these lands.

Although we have had many treaties and agreements with the governments that we deal with, time and time again those treaties and agreements were broken. However, our elders honored those treaties and agreements and took them to be sacred. But they discovered that the things that were written in the treaties and agreements were not what they had been led to believe were in them. I used to interpret for the elders because many of them did not speak or understand the English language, and they would tell me repeatedly that the things that are in the treaties were not the things that they had agreed to. I speak both English and Blackfoot languages fluently, yet I still have difficulty in getting across to the elders that I interpret for an accurate understanding of what is being said. What kind of interpreters did they have in those days when the treaties were being made? I have little doubt there were things that our elders were made to believe were in the treaties that are not there.

Our people have often had their hopes raised that things will improve, but always they have been disappointed. When a new administration takes office, then our people hope that it will do something for the Indian people. When the government sends people out into Indian country to find out what the Indian people want, the people again hope that something will happen. When the new regional and national Indian organizations were formed and the leaders tried to deal with our problems, then our people hoped that this would be a way of solving some of the problems and concerns that Indian people have. But still we find ourselves back at the bottom of the totem pole because always there were people giving the directions who were responsible to someone other than the Indian people.

When the Indian Reorganization Act of the United States was first introduced, our elders at that time questioned it, and most of the elders voted against bringing us under its jurisdiction. But the act was brought in anyway. The government may have thought that this particular act would cause Indian peoples to go out of existence. But they were wrong. They made a mistake when they forced Indian children to go to schools and learn their way. Those Indians who took advantage of the education are the very people who took the lead and began to turn things around for us. They began to take a hard look at the kinds of things that were coming down to the Indian people. Before that, our leaders unquestionably accepted the kinds of things that came down to them.

The tribes in the United States today have been confronted with just about everything. The government has come at us with many programs, different kinds of legislation, always with the promise that they were going to solve the problems that we are struggling with. In the end, however, we find that these policies were designed to assimilate us. For example, many of the tribes in the United States came under what was known as the Allotment Act, whereby individual members were given portions of tribal lands as their own private property. This was a way of making us lose the lands that we occupy. In later years they came up with what my people referred to as 'forced patents,' which allowed individual Indians to take their allotment of land out from under government trust. In other words, it was just like anyone else's land; they could sell it at any time. This was just another move designed to make our lands go out of existence.

There was also a program called 'relocation.' Under this legislation the government relocated our people, especially our young family members, into the metropolitan areas. Our young people were told that this is where the jobs are. This is where they would find the good life. A few of our people stayed and made a go of it. But for most it was a terrible tragedy. A story is told about a church pastor who came to an Indian fellow. Evidently this Indian was in need of a drink, and he went to the pastor for money so he could buy another drink. The pastor said to him, 'You know, I have been helping you out with money here and there for some time, but I never see you in church. You are going to have to start coming to church again, because if you don't you will go to that place for those people who don't go to church. That place is always hot, crowded, smelly, and dirty.' He went on and on, and made it sound awful. The Indian fellow stood there and listened to it all; then he said, 'Yes, I believe I know what you mean. Isn't that what they call relocation?'

These are a few examples of the different things we have been faced with, but we have withstood all attempts to eliminate our people and have moved forward, preserving and maintaining our Indian way of life. Many people misunderstand us when we talk about wanting to live the life of our ancestors. They think that we want to go back in time and live in our tepees, to be in our Indian costumes all year round, and to get away from what we have today. Indian people today want to maintain those traditions that they are able to. Our dance, song, language, arts, and crafts are the kinds of things that our people want to continue practising and showing their younger people. But at the same time we want our young people to do the kinds of things that they feel are going to help their people develop their communities and fulfil their desires. Today many of our young people are taking advantage of the things that are being made available to them in the larger society. They are not satisfied any longer simply to follow the white man. Nor do they want to dominate. Instead they are insisting on walking together as equals with those who have dominated us. They want to be able to have the same opportunities and be able to have the same benefits. They have a lot to offer and there are many instances where we can help one another.

Recently, my council bought space in a magazine to advertise our pencil factory. In it we said, 'We don't want your help, but we want your business.' The reason for this is that too often we are marked as people who always want hand-outs. Non-Indians don't realize that we have the desire and the potential to succeed, to build something that we can look to with pride and call ours. They have difficulty accepting that our business enterprises can be competitive with any other similar business operations in this country. Our pencil factory is successful. We hope that our product will be accepted like that of any other non-Indian industry.

We hope non-Indians will be willing to recognize that the products we put out are just as good as those being made elsewhere. Significantly, the Indian people who have made this factory into a success had no education, no training, yet today they are experts. It makes them very proud and lifts them up. It helps other Indians because they see that it can be done.

Today there are many important decisions to be made by Indian tribes. We must decide where we as Indian people want to go. We do not know what plans the federal government has for us Indian peoples. The leaders of the United States government say that they have our best interests at heart, yet we distrust their intentions. We must get our message and goals across to those government leaders. This is why at this time it is of vital importance for Indian people to join together in dealing with the government.

The 1980s are the years for being realistic. We can no longer pretend that grave dangers do not exist for our people and our culture. We must take a look at what we stand for. I believe in a statement that was made by one of our lawyers in Washington, DC. One of our elders asked him, through me as an interpreter, 'Why are our treaties broken? Why are they not lived up to by the government?' The lawyer said, 'When the white men came to this continent, you Indian people outnumbered them. There were more of you people, and you were powerful. They had to do something to avoid a war, so they pretended to make some kind of treaty to keep you peaceful. As the white men became stronger and many in numbers, they could care less about those treaties. Today they are so strong and great that they can break these treaties at will.' Unfortunately, this is true. But we must not stop our struggle.

As our elders have said, 'In the future you are going to continue fighting, not with bows and arrows but with documents, because again our adversaries will want our lands and what is under our land. They want it, and they will try to get it.' We are going to have to make a stand. We are going to have to depend on our leaders to keep our lands and to keep our traditional ways, our culture. It is going to take leadership and co-operation. That is the kind of stand that we must begin to make, whether we are Bloods, North Peigans, North Blackfoot, or Flathead. We are Indian people. As my people say, 'We are the real people.' We must fight for what the real people represent.

SOL SANDERSON

Preparations for Indian Government in Saskatchewan

The constitutional issue in Canada forced Indians and non-Indians alike to come to grips with the idea of Indian government. This issue has advanced the cause of Indian government in Canada immeasurably. There is nothing that my people in Saskatchewan could have done to focus attention so effectively on Indian government as was done by the constitutional issue. Our elders told us not to be afraid of the constitutional issue because Canada is like a baby. Non-Indians are only now starting to look at who they really are, why they exist in Canada. For the first time they are starting to relate to us, to sit down and talk with us. The constitutional issue forced them to recognize us as Indian people and to deal with our concerns.

What is the definition of Indian? For some purposes 'Indian' is defined as an ethnic group, just like Italians, French, or German. For other purposes 'Indian' is defined as a racial group like Blacks or Japanese. But in the Royal Proclamation, 'Indian' is defined as a nation. That definition is the basis of our claim to nationhood in Canada. The Federation of Saskatchewan Indians (FSI) is an assembly of nations. We have several bands that make up the Saulteaux nation, several bands that make up the Assiniboia nation, several bands that make up the Dakota Sioux nation, several bands that make up the Dene-Chippewyan nation, and several bands that make up the Cree nation. We also recognize that several of those nations extend beyond provincial boundaries. FSI is comprised of 69 Saskatchewan Indian bands. These bands range from 85 members to 3,000 members, and some bands have as many as 18 to 20 reserves. The 69 chiefs of the bands comprise the Regional Council of FSI. They meet four times a year for a full week to conduct research, develop Indian policy, and plan strategy.

It has been very difficult to structure a system in Saskatchewan that all tribes can relate to because not all tribes are governed by the same values and conditions. However, no matter which tribe we come from, there are protocol arrangements that we have agreed to. I refer to the rules that govern the deliberations of the chiefs when they enter the policy-conference rooms. For example, we still have the Sacred Stem, and we still have our Stem Keepers that protect and keep the Sacred Stem that was used at the time of the signing of the treaty.

To cover the vast territory over which Indians in Saskatchewan are dispersed, FSI has established seven district councils, which are comprised of chiefs representing the various nations and bands within those districts. It is in these district councils that the treaties are implemented. It is here that we formulate common goals and common policies.

Our reserved lands and the treaties we signed serve a special function in our claim to sovereignty as Indian nations. The reserved lands were secured for us and our future generations by our forefathers. They are termed reserved lands because title to those lands was retained by our forefathers and because they are still subject to Indian sovereignty. By signing treaties in Saskatchewan, we were guaranteed several different kinds of lands, not just reserved lands. We were guaranteed lands within treaty territory to ensure continued access to our traditional fishing and hunting grounds. We were also promised a land base for fishing stations, hunting, trapping, and gathering grounds. In this way our forefathers secured for us the right of access to the resources that we need for our living today. At the same time we are also seeking to expand our land base. There is nothing that prohibits us from expanding our land base – nothing in the treaties, for example, that says we cannot enlarge our land base. Consequently, expansion is one of our major objectives. We are at the moment selecting about 1.2 million acres of land for expansion. By the time we are finished, we estimate that we will have selected about 2.5 million acres of reserved lands over which we will declare Indian sovereignty.

Because the Europeans have been living here in Canada for some four hundred years, they have come to believe that they own some of our land and the resources on and under that land. We view these claims with concern and as an issue to be resolved by the federal, provincial, and Indian governments in Canada. In Saskatchewan we say that anything that was 'silent' at the time of negotiating treaty is still ours. In other words, anything that wasn't explicitly surrendered is still ours.

One of those areas that was silent at the time of negotiating treaty was mineral resources. We are now adhering to this silent principle in our negotiations on resource-sharing with the province of Saskatchewan. We are prepared to deal with all conflicting claims within a framework of sharing jurisdictional powers with the other governments. To this end we are currently working to establish our political sovereignty so that we can address the division of powers among the various levels of government in Canada. We want to establish clearly the jurisdictional powers of Indian government.

Most Europeans came to Canada in search of effective control over their political rights and their political institutions. This control had been denied to them in their mother countries. Their 'elders' no longer controlled the cultural and spiritual spheres of activity within their communities. These immigrants had also been denied effective control of their economy, their education, and their children. The symptoms of this loss of control were the very same as you observe among our native people here in Canada today: high suicide rates, serious alcohol problems, and high unemployment rates. If you want to see a contemporary European example of what I am talking about, go to East London, England. There you will find all of the conditions and symptoms I have just described. The reason for these cultural and social problems can be found in the total loss of control over virtually every aspect of their lives.

In Saskatchewan, Indians have decided to confront this problem by taking control over our communities and lives. In pursuing this objective we have encountered opposition from non-Indian people because the movement towards self-control by Indians is impacting on them. We are also getting resistance from our own people, but we are convinced that our first priority must be to take effective control over our own communities and lives. There are many approaches to it, many forms such control can take. I want to outline to you how we are approaching this objective in Saskatchewan.

People of different ethnic and cultural backgrounds can feel comfortable living in Canada in a melting-pot situation because they know that their mother country is always going to be fostering and preserving their culture, their language, and so on. It is not like that for us Indians. We have no place to retreat to. We have to stand firm where we are. So, in Saskatchewan, in exercising our trust obligations to future generations of Indians, our people and leaders are concentrating on safeguarding our cultural heritage.

As Indian people and Indian leaders we recognize that, for some time, the Canadian government has had a policy of termination for Indians. Evidence to this effect can be found in the 'detribalization policy' under which the government removed our children, at an early age, from the family unit. The policy objective of destroying the family unit was to destroy our community spirit. With the destruction of our community spirit, any kind of leadership in our community was negated. Recently the Canadian government has extended its strategy of liquidating Indians, by assimilation, to the fiscal arena. Through its fiscal policies the federal government seeks to eliminate all special programming and all special legislation dealing with Indians in Canada. This policy is designed actively to incorporate Indian people into the provincial economic, political, and social systems.

We are aware of the government's policies, and we are trying to counteract them by developing our own political institutions. We, the Federation of Saskatchewan Indians, have reorganized four times since 1944. Each reorganization had as its purpose to improve our capacity to accommodate to new policy developments, to strengthen our collective political alliances, to enhance our economic alliances, and to advance our cultural objectives.

In developing our political institutions during the past ten years, we have put great emphasis on strengthening the office of band chief. We often complain about government's disrespect for our chiefs, but we as Indian people are more to blame for that than anyone else. We had one hell of a task in Saskatchewan to get our people to give the chief's office the respect that it needs to function effectively. Our people tend to exploit that office when they need it but, at the same time, do not pay it adequate respect. So we have spent the past ten years developing the powers of the chief's office into the highest office of Indian government. In many instances we were opposed in this task by band-council members, because they were pawns of the Department of Indian Affairs.

When we started planning our political institutions, we identified four major functions to be served: educational development, economic development, social-cultural development, and political development. We still lack a true Indian policy to guide development in these areas, but our chiefs, sitting on policy boards, will continue to deliberate until a proper Indian policy is in place for each function.

At present there is a lack of accountability for Indian education in Saskatchewan. Neither the Department of Indian Affairs nor the provincial Education Department nor even FSI is responsible for Indian education. Consequently, we are now designing an organizational system, the Saskatchewan Indian Education Commission, that will be charged with responsibility to develop and provide quality Indian education. The commission will consist of elders who will control the curriculum and will be responsible for Indian administration of education.

For some time now we have recognized the critical importance of having our own educational institutions to counteract the influence of Canadian educational institutions on our young people, who are being alienated from their own communities and heritage. As Indian people we have been expected to change spiritually, culturally, and otherwise to conform to Canadian expectations. Non-Indian people seek to use their educational institutions to eliminate our uniqueness. The underlying reason for discrimination and the lack of understanding of Indians by non-Indians is that Canadian educational institutions fail to teach tolerance for uniqueness. When we emphasize cultural uniqueness in our classrooms, Indian Affairs officials threaten to reduce our budget because department officials object to our culture being taught in the school. If Canadian educational institutions will not teach their young tolerance for uniqueness, how can they learn to accept those who are different from themselves, in Saskatchewan, in Canada, and in the international community? We don't want our young people to become 'Canadian' in their thinking so that, when they return to their communities, they will advocate the federal government's policy goals from the inside. For this reason, in Saskatchewan we have set up several of our own educational institutions. We have the federated college, the community college, and the cultural college. Currently, we are developing the sports-college system.

In the area of economics, we have set up the Saskatchewan Indian Resource Council. The federal government has its economic policy. The province of Saskatchewan has its economic policy. We too want to have our Indian economic policy, whether it deals with environmental control, impact assessments, or industrial and business developments. We plan to take much greater control of resource developments than we have exercised in the past.

In the social-cultural sphere we have held a round of discussions with the appropriate provincial and federal government officials. We have organized a formal technical group that will be considering how to implement Indian law in the province of Saskatchewan and how to set up our Indian justice system, consisting of our own tribunals and bypassing the provincial judicial system. With respect to law in Canada, there currently exists the British common law, and that is based on title. We also have another law in Canada: the province of Quebec exercises what they call civil law. Indians are now saying that it is time we put in place Indian law, based on natural law. Not only Indians but all Canadians must accept the legitimacy of Indian law as it applies to our people. Canadians must become aware of Indian jurisdiction. They must respect the presence of Indian cultural activities, spiritual activities. Without recognition of our legal jurisdiction we will soon have no place to exercise any of our rights. I could go on about the number of social institutions that we are at present designing in an effort to build bridges among our people. We are *not* designing those Indian institutions to change Sioux to Cree, or Cree to Dene. We *are* creating those Indian institutions so that we can more effectively communicate and relate to each other.

In the political sphere we have established a Protectorate Office. This office has been created to ensure the protection of Indian people under the principles of international law against arbitrary action by the Canadian government. A commissioner working out of the Protectorate Office will monitor any new federal or provincial legislation that impacts on Indian rights or Indian lands. If the Indian people do not consent to the legislation, then it will be sent back for change to the appropriate legislature. Another function of the Protectorate Office is to set up tribunals to handle Canada-Indian disputes. Such disputes will always exist, no matter how perfectly the Constitution is designed. We are not prepared to continue going to the federal courts or the provincial courts to resolve 'Indian rights,' questions, and jurisdictional disputes. We contend that these disputes should be resolved either by all-Indian tribunals or by tribunals consisting of a membership half of whom would be appointed by the Indians and the other half by the federal government.

Indian peoples have never fully come to grips with the important issue of aboriginal rights. In this regard we have presented to the First Nations Assembly, the chiefs of Canada, a document called the 'Protocol–Aboriginal Concord Agreement.' It specifies that we, the aboriginal people of Canada, reserve the right to define aboriginal rights – not the Parliament of Canada, not the provincial legislature. It also provides for a protocol arrangement on how the Indian nations might associate and meet together in council. I regret to report that the First Nations Assembly has set that document aside. However, in Saskatchewan we take that document very seriously. It is important that, as the original peoples in Canada, we assert and protect our rights in this area. If we do not, somebody else will usurp what is rightfully ours. It may be the provinces or the territorial councils, or it may be the Parliament of Canada. The other office we are putting in place is the Treaty Enactment Office. This office will have responsibility not only for the treaties that deal with Crown-Indian relations but for those that may emerge between Indian nations in the future.

Also in the political sphere, we are exploring the idea of establishing an office to investigate the implications raised by those of our people who are interested in participating in the political institutions of Canada. We want to examine the terms of reference and benefits of that participation. It is likely that if there were a number of Indian MPs elected to Parliament or appointed to the Senate, the basic problems affecting Indians would be aggravated because government leaders would then consult them instead of coming to the true leaders of our people in Canada.

Finally in the political sphere, we have designed an Indian-government constitution to accommodate the broadest objectives possible, but the main objective is to protect individual band autonomy. Under this constitution each band will be allowed to regulate its own affairs with respect to cultural developments, spiritual developments, and language developments, and in developing any regulations that it wishes. In organizing our constitution, we will clearly spell out the division of powers for the bands. There will be powers delegated to the chiefs' council, to the elders' council, and to the chief and the headmen. In order to form our alliances politically, specified powers will be delegated to district councils, to the regional councils, to the First Nations Assembly, and to the chiefs' council of the First Nations at the national level.

That is the way we are designing our economic, social, and political systems. If there are better ways, I am sure we will find them.

DEL RILEY

What Canada's Indians Want and the Difficulties of Getting It

I was president of the National Indian Brotherhood (NIB) during the time of constitutional negotiations, and that time was punctuated with periods of emotion, tension, a tremendous amount of travel, and, I think, some progress.

In any political position or any position of responsibility you must develop a thick skin, or otherwise you are not going to last. You will not be able to handle the difficulties, the contradictions, the problems, the personal requests that you get from different people, and the conflicting situations in which you are constantly put. That is particularly true for Indian leaders in these difficult and emotional times. I have had ten years' experience in Indian politics in which not only to develop a thick skin but also to develop an understanding of the direction in which Indian people want to go.

One of the questions that is most commonly asked of me as I travel across Canada is, What do Indian people want? Why are you so concerned, they ask, about the Constitution? To answer those questions, I have said that Indian people in Canada are experiencing a reawakening. They have come of age. Indian people are saying that we are not satisfied with someone else shaping our future and running our affairs. Instead, we want a future that will take into account our spirituality and our traditional forms of government, that will allow us to live the kind of lives we desire.

The other thing that I tell Canadians, when they ask me what we Indians want, is that we seek basic human rights. We have regional differences, of course, but all across the country Indians are saying, 'We want basic human rights.' Sometimes it is termed 'self-determination.' Our quest for self-determination includes controlling those institutions that affect our lives. That is what Indian people are saying. Some Indian nations in Canada, of course, have gotten down to a lot more detail, a lot more substance as to what all of that means. But the basics of the Indian position and their goals are the same all across the country.

These were the goals that we pursued in the recent constitutional discussions. The role of the NIB was one of negotiation among Indian organizations, governments, and other institutions. This required confronting certain realities and making compromises. You can't just deal in philosophical or idealistic terms because you are dealing with very practical people out there, self-interested people with various kinds of motives. You are dealing with governments and institutions that have little in the way of conscience. This is what confronts Indians. Under these circumstances it was difficult, if not impossible, to get everything we wanted written into the Constitution.

The strategy pursued by the NIB was to act through political channels, and we applied various kinds of political pressures that we felt were effective in moving affairs in the direction of our goals. I think that one of the most important things we did was to take our case into the international arena. It was to our advantage that the chiefs of Canada went to England because it gave us an international forum, and it proved that Indian leaders are determined to take whatever action is necessary. The political impact of our activities in England was much greater than the Canadian government anticipated. The lobbying that we did over there has had significant results. Another important factor in our success in persuading the Canadian government to incorporate our position in the Constitution was the intense lobbying of Canadian parliamentarians that was done by Indian people. We lobbied far more intensively than we had done in the past in order to overcome the ignorance of Canada's political leaders on issues that affect our people. Sometimes they don't know what the issues are. They have other interests and other reasons for being in Parliament. We had to be certain that they understood the issues and our position. This required an educational process for them.

Our constitutional negotiations achieved some success. However, even if we had achieved everything we wanted in the Constitution, that wouldn't have meant the end of our battle. As a matter of fact, the battle would be just beginning. If we are going to have self-determination or

Indian government, there are many difficulties ahead, many obstacles, and we face the outright opposition of federal and provincial governments at all levels. If we want self-government, we are going to have to institute it on our own authority. It will not be accomplished by asking the Department of Indian Affairs if they will agree to Indian government or by negotiating self-determination at some conference with the Canadian government. What we must do is to plan our objectives and then, simply, carry them through. That is how we will achieve Indian government. This will not be easy.

The constitutional discussions created a lot of tension in the national Indian community. Different groups held different attitudes on what our position should be. The NIB was deeply involved in these ongoing debates within the Canadian Indian community, and, as a national political leader, I was placed in a cross-fire. One of the questions that was debated was, Why should we get involved in the constitutional discussions? Getting involved meant we had to deal with the Canadian government largely on its own terms. We had to weigh the implications of participating on such terms. After all, we are nations. Why should we stoop to ask the federal government for rights to which we have an inherent historical claim? But then again, would we have done the right thing for our people by staying away from the discussions? Had we not gotten involved in the discussions, the federal and provincial governments might have completely ignored our concerns. The NIB took the decision to participate in the constitutional discussions. We did so from the conviction that, as Indians, we had more to lose than gain by boycotting the discussions. If we, as Indians, want to claim nationhood status, then we must have relations with other nations. That includes Canada. We have been subjected to much criticism by some Indian leaders and groups for our decision, but what is wrong with negotiating for recognition from Canada? True, they occupy our land, but the reality is that it is a nation much more powerful than we are.

These are emotional times for Indian people, and sometimes our emotions cloud our thinking, to the detriment of achieving those objectives we seek. We must be very careful not to let emotions get in our way – not to let them cloud our rational movement towards our shared goals. In my judgment the NIB did develop a position on the Constitution that, generally speaking, accommodated all of the issues that had been presented to the national organization by member groups. At the same time our position was consistent with the positions taken by non-member native groups.

To achieve the kind of results that Indians want and expect, we require strong leadership and we need to support that leadership. After all, Indians have selected that leadership. Now, I know that there are mixed feelings in native communities about an elected leadership. But today we live in an age where we have to accept a lot of things that have been imposed on us, and it is tough. It is tough when the 51 per cent have to rule the 49 per cent. We immediately start out with opposing factions. This is a problem at every level of Indian decision-making: at the band-council level, at the provincial level, and at the national level. Opposition exists at every level. This has been one of our big weaknesses in the past, that we have always been vulnerable to the tactic of 'divide and conquer.' When we are divided, federal government politicians and bureaucrats can say, 'Your organization doesn't represent everyone,' or, 'That's not what the band chiefs say,' or, 'That's not what the Indian people say.' The element of unity has been missing from the national Indian movement.

Finally, one of the biggest problems we face, and I think it is something that we are beginning to solve, is our dependency on the federal government. I think this is one of the biggest attitude problems that we ourselves face. It is expressed by our people in a variety of ways. We have been indoctrinated for so many years to feel that we must always have someone else to depend on, someone else to do it for us. This sense of dependency among our people even extends to their attitude towards Indian organizations. We expect the organizations to do too much for us. It is time we began moving away from that dependency. In this regard I would like to paraphrase the words of one of the U.S. presidents: 'Ask not what your organization can do for you, but what you can do for your organization.' That challenge is going to have to be met in our attitudes towards Indian political organizations. Any political gains that we have made in the past have been the result of the political efforts of Indian people themselves. They have not been the product of the efforts of other people. We, the Indian people, have achieved whatever gains we now have, and, if we are to succeed in the future, we must continue to apply that principle. We must do it ourselves.

It is towards this end that the National Indian Brotherhood as a political organization tried to give leadership. As I saw it, it was the responsibility of the NIB to break down barriers on the road to Indian self-determination, the road to Indian government, the road to the ideal life that we all pursue. We are nations within Canada, and we have not given up our sovereignty. We have shared with Canada and have given all we can give. In order to meet our objectives, Canadians must now share with us.

SYKES POWDERFACE

Self-Government Means Biting the Hand That Feeds Us

Almost since the arrival of the Europeans, Indian people have been subjected to a foreign system. This system has met some of our needs, but for the most part the services have fallen far short of what is required and expected by Indian people. The main cause of our difficulties is to be found in Canadian political and legal institutions and the underlying values to which Indian people are subjected. These institutions and values are foreign to us. They do not conform to what Indian people have always lived by. We believe that if we are to survive as Indian people, we must return to our traditional institutions and values as prescribed by our elders and begin building our communities accordingly.

As a vice-president of the National Indian Brotherhood, I was extensively involved in the constitutional discussions. Very little of our initial position was accepted by the constitutional committee. This confirms my conviction that the political institutions of Canada are not really capable of accommodating the needs of aboriginal peoples. The constitutional process provided a good example of how the Canadian political and legal system functions to frustrate the aspirations of Indian people. Yet we survive, and we will continue to make progress in the face of serious obstacles so long as we build on those traditional values that our elders have taught us.

In all treaty areas, our band councils are the governments that deliver the bulk of services to band members. At present, very few bands have adequate government structures for delivering services to band members to meet their needs fully. If Indian government is going to meet the needs of band members adequately, it must not only have full control over band affairs but also be self-sufficient, and that takes money – white man's money.

Most treaty areas are organized as political units, with representation in Indian organizations at treaty-area, provincial, and national levels. These Indian organizations give the individual bands more political clout in their dealings with the federal and provincial governments. By working through such political organizations as the treaty-area councils, bands have been able to take over responsibilities for various services and programs from the Department of Indian Affairs. Where bands are small in size and population, these responsibilities may be better handled by regional Indian organizations instead of at the local level.

The Indian Affairs Branch (IAB) has not encouraged this progressive development of Indian government. There are regional councils being organized by our people, but these councils are subjected to IAB's concepts of what Indian government should be like. IAB officials are able to implement their ideas because the controlling factor is money, and the money always comes from the Canadian government. There are some bands that go it alone, but they have large land bases, large populations, and other resources under their control that yield the needed capital. When independently controlled resources (land, human, and financial) are present in an Indian community, real Indian government is feasible. Such bands can develop their communities to the point where they are no longer accountable to the federal government and no longer subjected to foreign ideas and a foreign system. They can develop their communities within a framework based upon those traditional values that the elders have taught us. They can become effective Indian governments, equipped to deal with problems that exist in their local communities.

Unfortunately, all of the funds that come from the federal government have strings attached, and this puts many bands or regional Indian councils into a position where they are accountable to IAB and not to their band members. This is a problem not only in the political field but also in the business field. When I was chief of the Stoney Reserve and administering my band's affairs, we had not only to fight for every dollar that we received from IAB, but every dollar had to be used only for those programs that the Branch developed and approved. The current move by the federal government to decentralize the decision-making authority to their regional offices represents no improvement in the problem. The money we receive from IAB regional offices has more strings attached than the dollars we used to get from Ottawa. The Branch has decentralized authority within its own system, but it has not increased the authority of Indian government. Through this retention of control, the department continues to implement and enforce its own policies, policies that do not reflect the aspirations or needs of the Indian people. It also places band councils and regional Indian councils in an impossible situation – between IAB and band members. Furthermore, IAB has created a situation of competition between treaty areas for scarce dollars. Thus, the Branch has been able to focus Indian attention on resource allocation and away from the serious problems inherent in its own bureaucracy. Through this tactic they have been able to side-track Indian bands and treaty areas from concentrating their energies into developing Indian government. Unless we find a solution to this problem, progress for Indian government will continue to be very slow.

Despite heavy departmental opposition and, in many cases, opposition from their own band members, Indian communities have made significant progress in developing Indian government since 1968. One of the assets that the Indian people have today is that they have become stronger in confronting IAB opposition. The stronger IAB opposition, the stronger Indian people seem to get. One of the strengths we have developed as Indian people has been education. Education is essential for developing Indian government. Combined with the experience we have gained, education has provided us with the necessary skills and knowledge to develop our own resources and to direct our own affairs. There are bands that are now ready for Indian government, but, unfortunately, not all bands are at that stage.

Today we confront a fundamental decision: whether treaty-area, provincial, and national levels of Indian government should declare their financial and political independence of the Canadian government. That is the crucial decision we must make. If we are going to be strong, if we are going to develop independent Indian government, we must first declare our financial independence. So long as we are financially dependent upon the federal government, we cannot chart our own paths and set our own goals. We must not be afraid to bite the hand that feeds us.

Many leaders at the band level have declared that the provincial and national Indian organizations ought to be accountable to their membership, not to the various agencies from which they receive their funding. I believe that the time has now come for bands to start considering what their responsibility is to the development of truly independent Indian organizations. They should give thought to pooling their financial resources to support their own political organizations, whether they be regional councils, treaty areas, or provincial or national organizations. That is where it is going to count, right at the spearhead. We Indian people must be willing to accept responsibility for supporting these political organizations financially in their efforts to achieve political independence. Otherwise our progress will be at the pace set by the federal government.

The Indian Association of Alberta is an example that we can use to drive home the significance of fiscal independence. Initially, when the Indian Association of Alberta was formed, it had no federal or provincial government monies. Financially it was independent. This was achieved by sacrifice. People worked for nothing because they saw the importance of developing Indian government, of not being controlled by the value system of someone else, of being motivated by their own value system. So they freely and willingly shared their time, their energy, and their talents. All of the work that was carried out was financed by individual and collective Indian contributions. The Indian Association of Alberta had remarkable strength at that time. Its members were not afraid to speak out against the federal and provincial governments on those issues that concerned Indian people. However, this changed completely when government monies were accepted to support the organization. The aggressiveness has been watered down, and compromises detrimental to our people have been made.

The time is now here when we have to answer some important questions. Are we going to continue to accept our funding from the Department of Indian Affairs? And the related question: Are our organizations going to continue functioning under the philosophies and the concepts of the Department of Indian Affairs? Are we going to continue being accountable to the Department of Indian Affairs at the expense of meeting the needs and expectations of our people? These questions have relevance for all the organizations from the local-band level on up to the national level. I believe it is time that we plan our own destiny in accordance with the traditional philosophies and values passed on by our elders. Remember, we have never relinquished our inherent right to self-determination, our right to Indian government. But to be able to claim this right, we must provide the necessary resources so that our organizations can achieve truly independent Indian government.

6 Indian Government and the Constitution

AS MUCH AS ANY OTHER single event during the past decade, the initial Constitutional Conference of First Ministers on the Rights of Aboriginal Peoples set the tone and parameters for the future development of self-government for Canada's native Indians. Significantly, the respective positions of each of the participant groups on the question of what increased self-government for natives means also became better articulated.

The conference was held pursuant to section 37 of the Constitution Act. This section stipulates that the prime minister must convene a meeting of first ministers and representatives of aboriginal peoples within a year after proclamation of the act to deal with constitutional matters that directly affect the aboriginal peoples of Canada, in particular aboriginal and treaty rights. The conference was the occasion of a face-to-face meeting between Canada's first ministers and the leaders of Canada's major aboriginal political organizations. The participant organizations were the Assembly of First Nations, the Native Council of Canada, the Métis National Council, and the Inuit Committee on National Issues.

The accomplishments of the conference on substantive issues were quite limited. The major achievement was a proposed constitutional amendment that is to be submitted by the first ministers to their respective legislatures. The proposed amendment contains three important provisions. First, the principle of equality between male and female persons with respect to aboriginal and treaty rights is to be confirmed. Second, rights acquired through existing and future land-claim settlements are to be constitutionally recognized. Finally, the amendment includes a commitment to a minimum of two future constitutional conferences to deal with issues relating to aboriginal peoples.

The conference clearly demonstrated the intensity of commitment by status Indians, who were represented at the deliberations by the Assembly of First Nations (AFN), to the principle that Indian government must be constitutionally entrenched as a distinct order of government in Canada. Of equal significance, federal officials revealed at the conference that they recognized the centrality of Indian government in future relations between status Indians and the rest of Canada. This was evident in the prime minister's opening remarks to the conference, in which he stated that 'the ... heart of the matter, the crux of our efforts to improve the condition of our aboriginal peoples and strengthen their relationships with other Canadians, is found within the set of issues concerning aboriginal government.' While the prime minister's remarks referred to the broader issue of self-government for all of Canada's aboriginal peoples, including Métis, Inuit, and non-status Indians, his remarks were of special significance to status Indians, who have lived under an externally imposed form of political and bureaucratic organization since the beginning of Confederation.

Finally, negotiations during the conference manifested the growing influence that Canada's provincial governments will have in the resolution of native issues. Historically, status Indians have shunned relations with provincial governments, fearing that the federal government would construe any alliance with the provinces as freeing it from its treaty obligations to Indians. However, the crucial role of the provinces in the new constitutional-amending process, coupled with their growing concern over Indian land claims and federal government initiatives to transfer financial responsibility for Indians to the provinces, has made them key players in the development of policies on Indian government.

Constitutional Entrenchment of Indian Government

The position of the AFN at the conference was for constitutionally based Indian government. They see such an arrangement as less vulnerable to legislative intrusion by Parliament and less susceptible to what Indian leaders consider to be the capriciousness of the Canadian political process. Band-level Indian leaders also believe that a constitutionally entrenched Indian government will protect them from judicial undercutting of their authority and will check the encroachment of provincial laws and regulations on their jurisdiction.

The drive by the AFN for constitutional entrenchment of Indian government evolves naturally from the long-standing demand of Indians for self-determination. The lexicon of Indian demands has, over the past decade, included terms such as self-determination and sovereignty as well as Indian government. In essence, these concepts have been used by Indian peoples to express a fundamental claim against the rest of Canada for the recognition of their cultural uniqueness and their inherent right to control their own destiny. In recent years these concepts have been subsumed by Indians under the more comprehensive notion of aboriginal rights, commonly referred to as the 'rights of first nations.' The term 'aboriginal rights' refers to a complex of political, social, economic, and cultural rights believed by Indians to be necessary for their survival as distinct peoples. Indian leaders insist that these rights must be constitutionally guaranteed.

It is worth noting that Indian leaders are not advocating entrenchment of a detailed organizational structure for Indian government. In fact, given the different political traditions of the various Indian bands, it is highly unlikely that a consensus could be achieved on a common form of Indian government. Instead, Indian leaders propose the entrenchment of a broad statement of principle that would allow Indian government to become operational in a variety of forms to fit the varying needs and traditions of Indian bands across Canada. As David Ahenakew, grand chief of the Assembly of First Nations, indicated in his opening remarks to the conference,

There is a wide range of options as to how we can, within the Canadian federation, exercise our jurisdiction and establish our own political, social and economic institutions. The Canadian Parliament must avoid the temptation to impose a uniform 'formula' on all Indian governments in Canada.

This argument, of course, reflects a historic reaction among Indians to the uniform requirements of the Indian Act with respect to the elective forms of band governments.

Indian leaders advocate that Indian government should be considered a 'first-order' government – that is, a government with guaranteed jurisdictional authority similar in type, although not necessarily in scope, to that of the provincial governments in their relationship to the federal government. This position finds expression in a constitutional amendment proposed by the AFN to section 35, part II, of the Charter of Rights and Freedoms. The amendment, entitled 'A Statement of Particular Rights of First Nations,' would add three rights:

1 The right of the First Nations to their own self-identity, including the right to determine their own citizenship and forms of government;
2 Their right to determine their own institutions;
3 The right of their governments to make laws and to govern their members and the affairs of their people and to make laws in relation to management, administration, and use of their lands and resources.

The Federal Government and Indian Government

The federal government took the opportunity at the constitutional conference to spell out its policy principles for the future development of Indian government. Speaking for the Canadian government, Prime Minister Trudeau unequivocally rejected political sovereignty for Indians. At the same time he also ruled out assimilation as an alternative model for dealing with native Indians. Trudeau's rejection of independence as a possible political status for Canada's Indian peoples is consistent with the federal government's broader attitude towards secessionist movements and is in line with past and present Indian policy. But his disavowal of assimilation as a policy goal, if genuine, represents a complete turn-about from the Trudeau-inspired 1969 White Paper.

The position taken into the conference by the Assembly of First Nations was for a *measure* of sovereignty and jurisdiction *within* Confederation. Not all Indian groups accept this position. The Iroquois Confederacy, for example, has historically insisted that it is a sovereign, independent nation in relationship to the Canadian state.

The federal government's readiness to negotiate a form of Indian government that falls between the extremes of political independence and assimilation is, at best, a vague policy position. In the past the federal government has rejected any suggestion of Indian government functioning parallel to or separate from other systems of government within Canada. The federal government has insisted that Indian government must fit into the existing division of powers between the provinces and the federal government – that is, that Indian government must be subordinate to the jurisdictional authority of the provinces and the federal government. Under such constraints the autonomy of Indian government would be severely limited.

The willingness of federal officials to include Indian government as an item on the agenda of future constitutional conferences should not be interpreted as a sign that the federal government favours constitutional entrenchment of Indian government. Support for entrenchment would represent a radical departure from the past and current policy position of the Department of Indian Affairs and Northern Development (DIAND). Since the mid-1970s DIAND has sought to create a *legislatively* based form of self-government for status-Indian bands. Under such an arrangement the authority of Indian government would continue to exist as a grant from Parliament.

At the same time that the constitutional discussions of Indian government were being conducted, a parliamentary subcommittee (of the Standing Committee on Indian Affairs and Northern Development) on Indian Self-Government was also conducting hearings with Indian political organizations and individual Indian bands on the subject of Indian government. This committee was mandated to review '... all legal and related institutional factors affecting the status, development and responsibilities of Band Governments on Indian reserves.' Ultimately, this committee is expected to make recommendations to Parliament that will form the basis of new legislation allowing greater political and administrative autonomy for band governments. The existence and mandate of the Subcommittee on Indian Self-Government leaves little doubt that the federal government continues to favour a legislative base for Indian government; however, it wants to assure that any accords that may emerge from pending constitutional negotiations will be consonant with the legislative provisions for Indian government. This analysis of federal government policy is consistent with the committee's charge to take into account the aboriginal- and treaty-rights section (section 35) of the Constitution Act and whatever other pacts emerge from the First Ministers' Conference on Aboriginal Peoples.

It appears, then, that in the future, federal policy regarding Indian government will be developed in an expanded policy-making arena. This arena will include constitutional conferences, the federal legislative and bureaucratic policy-making process, and federal-provincial negotiations.

Consistent with this new approach, the federal government has created an office of Aboriginal Constitutional Affairs. This agency, which will report to the Cabinet, is charged with co-ordinating all federal government activities related to the ongoing process of defining the rights of aboriginal peoples. It will guide research and policy development on aboriginal constitutional issues and advise the federal government on implementation. This office will complement existing administrative structures such as DIAND, and it will also work with the representatives of aboriginal peoples in planning for future constitutional conferences.

The federal government's strategy of expanding the policy-making arena will create serious difficulties for native Indian leaders in developing approaches to achieve a greater measure of self-determination. The presence of a number of different policy-making groups and levels with complex and ambiguous divisions of responsibility will overburden the already heavily taxed capacity of native peoples to develop and advance their models of self-government effectively.

Indian Government and the Provinces

The proceedings of the constitutional conference underlined the growing but as yet undefined powers of the provinces in deciding the future of Indian government. The fact that the provinces, under the Constitution, are required to participate in the definition of aboriginal rights guarantees them an important role in the development of Indian government.

Even apart from their formal, constitutionally required participation in the definition of aboriginal rights, provincial involvement in Indian affairs has expanded significantly over the past decade. This involvement today includes providing services in health, education, and social welfare, especially to off-reserve–dwelling Indians, and increased assistance for economic development on reserves, with emphasis on business and agriculture. The provinces have also increasingly engaged in jurisdictional disputes with Indian bands, not only over traditional concerns, such as hunting, fishing, and water rights, but also in regard to social issues, such as adoption and child welfare. Moreover, the provinces are concerned about Indian land claims and their impact on provincial revenues stemming from resource exploitation and other forms of economic activity. Another example of the expanded interest of the provinces in

Indian affairs can be found in the growing number of provincial government structures that have been created for the purpose of policy-making and the delivery of services to Indian peoples. These structures range from cabinet portfolios and secretariats to divisions within regularly operating government departments.

Provincial officials are apprehensive of attempts by the federal government to shift financial responsibility for status Indians to the provinces. This anxiety is well grounded. Indian peoples are in a position comparable to that of developing nations: they are in need of technical and administrative assistance as well as economic support. If the federal government continues its current policy of fiscal restraint, the provinces are likely to find themselves responsible for the shortfall – that is, the provinces could find themselves having to commit significant amounts of their own fiscal and other resources to underwrite the cost of emerging Indian government.

Another consideration for the provinces pertains to the future application of section 91(24) of the Constitution Act. This section gives responsibility for Indians and Indian lands to Parliament. Should a new order of Indian government develop under federal legislation, the provinces will be confronted with a situation where, on the one hand, they are being asked to increase their financial commitment to Indian government while, on the other, their jurisdiction over Indians and their control over expenditure of provincial funds by Indians remain ambiguous. The provinces, understandably, balk at funding programs under these conditions, and they insist on attaching conditions regarding the use of their funds by Indians.

Ironically, the same concern, although in a reverse form, faces status Indians. While Indians desperately need and want the economic, technical, and administrative assistance that the provinces have to offer, they know that acceptance of such assistance means more intrusion into their affairs by the provinces. They also fear that increased involvement with and by the provinces, especially in the process of defining aboriginal rights, will jeopardize the historic trust-relationship that Indians hold with with the federal government. It could undermine their special status under section 91(24) of the Constitution Act. This fear underlies Indian opposition to provincial participation in any negotiations on the subject of aboriginal rights.

Ultimately, the attitude of the provinces towards the development of Indian government will hinge largely upon three considerations: 1 / the size of the financial commitment they will be asked to assume; 2 / the control they will have over the use of those funds; and 3 / the extent to which they have jurisdiction over Indians and their lands. It is unrealistic to expect anything but a cautious approach until the provinces fully understand the implications of Indian government for provincial authority and jurisdiction.

Concluding Observations

The effectiveness of status-Indian leaders in bargaining with federal and provincial officials for a new order of Indian government for their people rests largely upon factors intrinsic to the aboriginal peoples themselves. Two of these factors are of major importance in the political negotiations that lie ahead. First, the capacity of Indian leaders to be consistent and effective in their negotiations with the other governments in Canada depends largely on the measure of intragroup support they receive from their constituents. At the initial constitutional conference, the federal government accepted the Assembly of First Nations as being representative of status Indians, and it is likely to continue this stand in future conferences. However, the political acceptability of the Assembly of First Nations within the status-Indian community is far from assured; the policy positions taken by the AFN on Indian government are subject to factional tendencies within its membership and to the counter-forces of provincial Indian associations. A number of Indian bands, as well as some provincial Indian associations, have recently developed their own constitutional committees for developing policy positions. Several of their briefs were tabled at the first constitutional conference. In part, such moves reflect a desire for greater involvement by local Indian communities. However, the effect of such involvement is to exacerbate the problem of achieving a policy consensus in the Indian community.

The situation that the AFN faces with respect to its membership underscores a fundamental truth about status Indians across Canada: despite the fact that status Indians have been treated collectively for administrative purposes under the Indian Act, they remain a culturally and politically diverse group of peoples. Indian peoples do not consider themselves *one* nation but rather many *nations*; some bands are wealthier and larger than others and, therefore, see greater advantage in moving towards increased political and administrative autonomy. Any new order of Indian government in Canada will have to accommodate the cultural, political, and economic diversity of Canada's Indians. The federal government's proposed, legislatively based Indian government model recognizes *economic* diversity, by allowing bands to opt in or out, but fails to recognize the *cultural* and *political* diversity of Canada's Indians in any meaningful way.

Given the lack of consensus in the Indian community on the form and jurisdiction of pan-Indian government, it is reasonable to expect that Indian government will initially emerge at the band level. Ironically, the development of more political autonomy by Indians at the band level may undercut the capacity of provincial and national political organizations such as the AFN to act as spokesorganizations for the collective interests of status Indians. The decline of provincial and national Indian organizations is especially likely once agreements have been worked out on the major collective concerns, such as aboriginal and treaty rights. It is problematic whether the AFN has a future political or administrative role at a pan-Indian level of government.

A second factor, intrinsic to the Indian community, that will prove influential in their ability to bargain effectively with the other Canadian governments concerns the readiness of Canada's three major aboriginal groups to maintain an intergroup common front vis-à-vis the federal and provincial governments in their political negotiations. If factionalism develops among the Métis, Inuit, non-status, and status Indians, it could undermine the bargaining position of each group. The four groups were able to maintain unity during the initial constitutional conference, but that meeting dealt mainly with the holding of future meetings, and they shared a joint interest in having future meetings. However, the alliance could readily disintegrate when substantive issues are being considered. Due to the varying historical experiences and circumstances of each native group and because of the different relationship each group currently has to the federal and provincial governments, each starts from a different baseline in seeking to achieve self-determination.

Among the several groups, status Indians and Inuit are closest to each other in their approaches. Both have identifiable land areas that can provide a territorial base for self-government. The Inuit, moreover, were classified as Indian by the Supreme Court in 1939. This ruling placed them under federal jurisdiction and made them eligible to receive federal financial support. The Métis, however, do not have an identifiable land base. Furthermore, their relationship has been primarily with the provincial governments.

The provincial governments, particularly those of the prairie provinces, see the Métis as a provincial responsibility. In his opening statement at the constitutional conference, the premier of the province of Alberta indicated clearly that Alberta's primary concern is its responsibility to the Métis within its borders. In fact, Alberta has already provided a type of land base for Métis settlements under the Métis Betterment Act. However, in its presentation to the conference, the Métis National Council argued that the Métis should become a federal responsibility and have constitutionally guaranteed 'self-government, which shall have jurisdiction over political, cultural, economic and social affairs and institutions deemed necessary to their survival and development as a distinct people.' The Manitoba Métis Federation in its brief argued that 'the Constitution must ensure that federal financial responsibility has applicability to the needs of the Métis as well as to other aboriginal peoples.' In short, the Métis regard their constitutional identification as one of the aboriginal peoples to mean that they should be treated in the same way as the status Indians and the Inuit.

There is little doubt that the historical, legal, and political differences among the aboriginal groups will produce differing policy goals during future negotiations over the meaning of aboriginal rights and self-government. This division will occur against the backdrop of a federal-provincial tug-of-war for jurisdiction over Indians and Indian lands, while, at the same time, each will want to eschew increased financial responsibility for natives. If aboriginal peoples are to achieve a measure of self-determination, each constituent group must recognize the importance of support for its leadership. Also, the leadership of each major group must recognize the importance of maintaining a common front and be prepared to make the necessary compromises for unity.

APPENDIXES

LIST OF CONTRIBUTORS

Indian Government Pursuant to the Indian Act

Indian government is not something that has developed recently. Indian government has been in existence for as long as the Indian peoples of North America have been in existence. Recently, however, the term 'Indian government' has been used by both Indians and government officials in Canada as an umbrella concept to articulate their respective political objectives. The Indian people consider Indian government to mean greater autonomy and constitutional recognition of their right to self-determination. Because Indian government has a positive value for Indian people, the federal government is characterizing its proposed revisions or amendments to the Indian Act as 'Indian-government legislation.' But the Indian Act is basically an administrative act and offers little scope for real, substantive governing powers by Indians. When Indians speak of Indian government, they talk in terms of the substantive powers they held as first nations, prior to colonization. Thus, there is quite a gap in understanding between Indians and government officials with respect to the meaning of Indian government. This difference contributes to a wide communication and policy chasm between government officials and Indian peoples.

Background of Indian Government

To understand Indian government under Indian Act legislation, it is necessary to understand the goal of Canadian Indian policy. Canadian Indian policy has historically been geared towards assimilation. From the beginning the Canadian government has consistently sought to assimilate Indians into the dominant society. This objective is evidenced

in the following statement by William Sprague, who was deputy superintendent of Indian Affairs in the 1870s:

The Acts framed in the years 1868 and 1869 relating to Indian Affairs, were
designed to lead the Indian people by degrees to mingle with the white race
in the ordinary avocations of life. It was intended to afford facilities for electing, for a limited period, members of bands to manage, as a Council, local
matters; that intelligent and educated men, recognized as chiefs, should carry
out the wishes of the male members of mature years in each band, who
should be fairly represented in the conduct of their internal affairs. Thus
establishing a responsible, for an irresponsible system, this provision, by law,
was designed to pave the way to the establishment of simple municipal institutions.[1]

In the beginning Indians resisted imposition of the provisions of the
Indian Act that required them to constitute an elected council. Some
bands continue to challenge the authority of the Indian Act. For example, the St Regis Mohawks proclaim that they are sovereign and
not subject to Canadian legislation. However, in spite of this resistance,
an elected form of government has been established on the St Regis
Indian reserve and exists alongside the traditional Indian council. The
question as to which government or council is the legitimate one has
been the subject of legal disputes. The courts have held in favour of
the council elected in accordance with the provisions of the Indian
Act.

On the Plains, many Indian bands *seemingly* adopted an Indian Act
form of Indian government; however, this must be placed in context.
Traditionally, Plains Indian tribes selected chiefs on the basis of their
charismatic and other leadership qualities. They appointed their chiefs
for specific purposes, such as hunting, conducting war, or migrating, and
so on. When the Indian Act form of elected government was imposed on
them, they simply elected those leaders that they would have asked to lead
the tribe under their traditional customs. So, superficially, it appeared as
though many tribes on the Plains had adopted the Indian Act political
system. In fact, they hadn't really adopted the system; they had merely
adapted it to their traditional way of selecting chiefs. Today, however,
the electoral provisions of the Indian Act have become institutional-
ized in the majority of reserves across the Prairies. For these bands the
electoral system, with its characteristic style of political recruitment,

has largely replaced the traditional charismatic approach to selecting leaders.

Indian Government and the Indian Act

The electoral provisions of the Indian Act stipulate that each band can elect one chief and one councillor for every one hundred persons, to a maximum of twelve councillors. So, in effect, a band council can consist of a maximum of thirteen people (one chief and twelve councillors).

Indian Act councils are elected in accordance with sections 74 and 75, which read as follows:

Whenever he deems it advisable for the good government of a band, the Minister may declare by order that after a day to be named therein, the Council of the Band, consisting of a Chief and Councillor, shall be selected by elections to be held in accordance with this Act.

Section 75 of the act spells out the criteria of eligibility to run for band council. Section 75 of the Indian Act states that:

1 No person other than an elector who resides in a section may be nominated for the office of councillor to represent that section on the council of the Band.
2 No person may be a candidate for election as chief or councillor unless his nomination is moved and seconded by persons who are themselves eligible to be nominated.

Basically, this section of the act requires that a person running for council has to be an elector. An elector is a person who is a member of a band, who is at least twenty-one years of age, and is not disqualified from voting at band elections. There are no similar criteria or conditions for a person to run for chief. Presumably, that means that a non-band member may run for chief of an Indian band. However, a person who stands for chief must be nominated by a person who is eligible to be nominated for band council.

A distinction must be made between a band council that is constituted under the electoral provisions of the Indian Act and a council that has been elected according to 'custom,' as provided under the Act. There is a general misunderstanding of what is meant by custom in this instance.

Custom under the Indian Act and as used by the Department of Indian Affairs does not refer to any particular traditional manner of electing councils. Custom simply means a system of electing a council according to rules established by a band, and that system may or may not be based on a traditional way of electing or choosing leaders. Custom simply refers to those councils which are elected by other than the Indian Act elective system. An Indian band that conducts its elections for council under the provision of custom can make different rules and regulations with regard to who is eligible for chief, who is eligible for council, and how the elections for chief and council may be conducted. They may also change the number of councillors that would make up the band council.

The powers of a band council are spelled out in section 81 of the Indian Act. These are basically the powers to make by-laws. Band councils can pass by-laws on the following matters:

a for the health of residents on the reserve and to prevent the spreading of contagious and infectious disease;

b for the regulation of traffic;

c for the observance of law and order;

d for the prevention of disorderly conduct and nuisances;

e for the protection against and prevention of trespass by cattle and other domestic animals, the establishment of pounds, the appointment of pound keepers, the regulation of their duties and the provision for fees and charges for their services;

f for the construction and maintenance of water courses, roads, bridges, ditches, fences and other local works;

g for the dividing of the reserve or portion thereof into zones and the prohibition of the construction or maintenance of any class of buildings or the carrying on of any class of business trade or calling in any such zone;

h for the regulation of the construction, repair and use of buildings, whether owned by the band or by individual members of the band;

i for the survey and allotment of reserve lands among the members of the band and the establishment of a register of Certificate of Possession and Certificates of Occupation relating to allotments and the setting apart of reserve lands for common use, if authority therefor has been granted under section 60;

j for the destruction and control of noxious weeds;

k for the regulation of bee keeping and poultry raising;

l for the construction and regulation of the use of public wells, cisterns, reservoirs and other water supplies;
m for the control and prohibition of public games, sports, races, athletic contests and other amusements;
n for the regulation of the conduct and activities of hawkers, peddlers or others who enter the reserve to buy, sell or otherwise deal in wares or merchandise;
o for the preservation, protection and management of fur bearing animals, fish and other game on the reserve;
p for the removal and punishments of persons trespassing upon the reserve or frequenting the reserve for proscribed purposes;
q with respect to any matter arising out of or ancillary to the exercise of powers under this section; and
r for the imposition on summary conviction of a fine not exceeding $100 or imprisonment for a term not exceeding 30 days or both for violation of a by-law made under this section.

In addition to the above by-law–making powers, the governor-in-council, under section 83, may declare that the band has reached an 'advanced state of development,' and the council of the band may therefore, subject to the approval of the minister, make by-laws for any or all of the following purposes:

a the raising of money by 1 / the assessment and taxation of interests in land in the reserve of persons lawfully in possession thereof, and 2 / the licensing of businesses, callings, trades and occupations;
b the appropriation and expenditure of moneys of the band to defray band expenses;
c the appointment of officials to conduct the business of the council, prescribing their duties and providing for their remuneration out of any moneys raised pursuant to paragraph a;
d the payment of remuneration in such amount as may be approved by the Minister to chiefs and councillors, out of any moneys raised pursuant to paragraph a;
e the imposition of a penalty for non-payment of taxes imposed pursuant to this section, recoverable on summary conviction not exceeding the amount of the tax or the amount remaining unpaid;
f the raising of money from band members to support band projects; and

g with respect to any matter arising out of or ancillary to the exercise of
powers under this section

All band councils have the by-law–making powers stipulated under
section 81. However, only a few Indian bands have been declared by the
governor-in-council to have achieved an advanced stage of development
and, therefore, to have become entitled to pass money or tax by-laws
under section 83. The Department of Indian Affairs has not made public
the criteria for determining whether or not a particular band has reached
an advanced stage of development, so what is meant by this term, and
how it is determined that a particular band has reached that stage, is not
publicly known.

In addition to the powers that a band council may exercise under sections 81 and 83 of the act, the minister of Indian Affairs has discretionary
authority to grant powers in the form of 'consent to act.' Probably the
most important band-council power of this kind is the power to allot
lands under section 20 of the Indian Act. Section 20(1) states:

No Indian is lawfully in possession of land in a reserve unless, with the
approval of the Minister, possession of the land has been allotted to him by
the council of the band.

Under this section the band council is empowered to divide up reserve
lands for the exclusive use of and occupation by tribal members.

Other sections of the Indian Act permit the minister, with the consent
of the band council, to adjust contracts entered into by the band with
outside parties. Examples of this would be leases by outsiders of reserve
lands for agricultural use, agreements with non-Indians for exploitation
of natural resources, and the expenditure of capital and revenue money.
In most cases the minister has the final authority, even when the Indian
Act states that the band must be consulted with regard to a particular
action that the minister may want to take.

A very important and unsettled issue of contemporary Indian government revolves around the legal status of an Indian band and, consequently, the legal status of a band council. An opinion rendered by the
Department of Justice has resulted in the refusal of the Department of
Indian Affairs to recognize Indian bands as having legal status. This is
the policy despite the fact that the Department of Indian Affairs, in its

own position papers, has itself recommended recognizing Indian bands as having legal status. Where the issue of legal status has come to the attention of the court, Indian bands have, in some decisions, been recognized as possessing legal status. For instance, in a case just recently heard in Alberta involving the question of whether or not provincial labour laws apply on an Indian reserve, the judge held that, because a band is an entity that enters into agreements with other legal entities, it has legal status, and, therefore, the provincial labour laws must apply to that band. Another interesting situation is that the Income Tax Act of Canada recognizes an Indian band as a municipality for the purposes of donations made to that band. Still other cases have held that an Indian band is a legal entity for purposes of civil suits.

Indian Government and the Constitution

One cannot talk about Indian government without referring to the new Canadian Constitution and its implications for Indian government. There are basically three different political positions that native people can adopt with regard to the Constitution:
1 they can assume a sovereign position of complete autonomy from the Canadian government;
2 they can take the position of a constitutionally recognized government within the Canadian constitutional framework; or
3 they can maintain the status quo – that is, continue to operate under the present Indian Act.
Each approach would have a significantly different implication for Indian band government. If the first position, that of sovereignty, were taken, that would mean that Indians would have complete autonomy to form their own governments and pass their own laws. If the second position, that of a constitutionally recognized government equivalent to a provincial government, were pursued, that would mean another order of government in addition to the federal and provincial governments now in place. If such an order of government were to come into existence, it would require the spelling-out of the substantive powers that Indians would exercise under such an order of government. An implication of such a move would be to recognize that Indians are sovereign and are entering Confederation in much the same way that Newfoundland joined Confederation in 1949.

If the third position, that of maintaining the status quo, were taken, it would mean that the current legislative approach to Indian government would be continued. The federal government, pursuant to section 91(24) of the Constitution Act, would have to pass legislation allowing Indian tribes to form a government pursuant to whatever the new legislation says. That form of government – that is, a legislatively based government – would necessarily be a municipal form of government. Many Indian tribes do not want municipal-government status because they associate municipalities with provincial jurisdiction, and most Indian tribes and bands do not want to come under provincial jurisdiction. They interpret that as a termination of the historical special status of Indian bands and as meaning the loss of all their treaty and aboriginal rights. Indians want a 'government-to-government' relationship. Such a relationship would imply internal autonomy for both governments. It would mean that Indians could pass whatever laws they desired and could determine the nature of their relationship with Canada.

Whatever kind of Indian government emerges from the new Constitution Act, one very important factor has to be kept in mind: in Canada, because of parliamentary supremacy, there is no such thing as constitutional law. A constitution is an instrument that puts certain limitations on government and on the powers or authority that a government can exercise. So long as parliamentary supremacy is in place in the Canadian system of government, parliamentary supremacy will always override constitutional law. Therefore, we can conclude that there is not much distinction between what is constitutional, what is legislative, and what is a regulatory scheme. If we look at these three levels of law in Canada, we find that in some cases legislation overrides what should normally be considered constitutional law. In some cases a regulation overrides legislation, and in some cases regulation even overrides constitutional law. Thus, there is not much difference in actual impact or application whether Indians get self-government through constitutional law or through legislation or through a regulatory scheme. Accordingly, from an Indian perspective, it would seem that the best strategy to achieve Indian government is to pursue it on all levels and from all sides rather than to concentrate all efforts in one political approach.

It is difficult to say with certainty what the precise form of Indian government that will emerge from the current activity and negotiations will be. In 1980, the Research Branch of the Department of Indian Affairs produced a report entitled *Government under Indian Act Legislation, 1868– 1951*. Reading this report, it is easy to be cynical about the current activities taking place with regard to Indian government, because the model advocated in the report is no different from the government that Indians have had for the past hundred years. Whatever comes out of the new efforts with regard to Indian government, whether it is legislatively based or entrenched in the Constitution Act, we can safely assume that the final result will not be very different from the form prescribed by the existing Indian Act provisions for Indian government.

LEROY LITTLE BEAR

Note

1 Deputy Superintendent William Sprague to Secretary of State Joseph Howe, 2 Feb 1871; quoted in Wayne Daugherty and Dennis Madill *Indian Government under Indian Act Legislation* (Ottawa: Department of Indian and Northern Affairs 1980) p 2

APPENDIX II

Selected Demographic Information on Status Indians

Total status-Indian population: 292,700
Number of bands: 573
Land area of reserves: 26,525 sq kilometres
Band size:

% of population in each band-size group (1977)

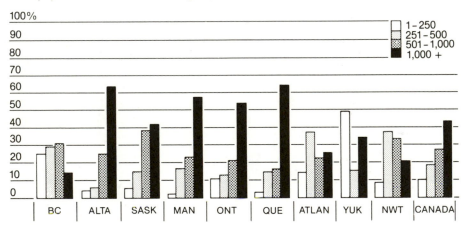

Source: Indian Conditions: A Survey (Ottawa: Canada Department of Indian Affairs and Northern Development 1980)

Status Indians living on
  reserves (1980):   71%
Status Indians living off
  reserves (1980):   29%

193 Selected Demographic Information on Status Indians

Status-Indian population by province:

Newfoundland	1,010
PEI	400
Nova Scotia	5,905
New Brunswick	4,235
Quebec	34,400
Ontario	70,190
Manitoba	39,710
Saskatchewan	37,470
Alberta	35,810
British Columbia	54,085
Yukon	2,770
NWT	6,720

Source: Government of Canada, information furnished for the Constitutional Conference of First Ministers on the Rights of Aboriginal
Peoples 1983

Federal Programs and Services for Status Indians 1982–3

Total federal expenditures: $1,582,000
South of 60 degrees latitude: 1,492,000
North of 60 degrees latitude: 90,000
Per capita expenditures for
   status Indians on reserves: 6,330
Federal expenditures for status Indians
  (south of 60 degrees) by program area 1982–3:

Program area	$ millions	%
Education	436.0	29.2
Social services	270.5	18.1
Health	204.9	13.7
Culture	18.9	1.3
Justice	2.0	0.1
Housing and community infrastructure	215.4	14.4
Employment and economic development	123.5	8.3
Band government	67.8	4.5
Miscellaneous	47.7	3.2
Administrative overhead	105.3	7.1
Total:	$1,492.0	100.0

Source: Government of Canada, information furnished for the Constitutional Conference of First Ministers on the Rights of Aboriginal Peoples 1983

Contributors

Oren Lyons is subchief of the Turtle clan of the Iroquois nation and professor of American Studies at the University of Buffalo, Buffalo, New York.

Tom Porter is chief of the Bear clan of the Mohawk nation and an internationally known lecturer and speaker on North American Indian culture and philosophy.

Rudolph C. Ryser is special assistant to the president of the World Council of Indigenous Peoples; a member of the Cowlitz tribe, he has served as a political adviser to a number of Indian tribes and organizations in the United States.

Marie Smallface is chief administrator for the World Council of Indigenous Peoples and a lecturer in the Department of Native American Studies, University of Lethbridge; a member of the Blood tribe, she was a staff person with the National Indian Brotherhood from 1973 to 1975.

Kirke Kickingbird is executive director of the Institute for the Development of Indian Law in Washington, DC, and a noted lawyer and spokesman for Indian legal rights.

David Nicholson has been assistant deputy minister of Indian Affairs and Northern Development in the government of Canada and director-general of Indian Affairs and Northern Development for the provinces of Manitoba and Alberta.

Sally M. Weaver is a professor of Anthropology at the University of Waterloo and author of *Making Canadian Indian Policy: The Hidden Agenda 1968–70.*

H.W. Thiessen is the managing director of the Native Secretariat of the government of Alberta.

Andrew Ebona is executive director for the Central Council of the Klinkit and Haida tribes of Alaska and former executive director of the National Congress of American Indians.

John D. Whyte is a professor of Law at Queen's University and formerly director of the Constitutional Law Branch of the Saskatchewan Department of the Attorney-General.

Douglas E. Sanders is a professor of Law at the University of British Columbia, consultant to the Assembly of First Nations and to the Native Council of Canada, legal counsel to the World Council of Indigenous Peoples, and author of numerous articles on Indian legal rights.

J. Rick Ponting is a professor of Sociology at the University of Calgary and co-author of *Out of Irrelevance: A Socio-Political Introduction to Indian Affairs in Canada*.

Roger Gibbins is a professor of Political Science at the University of Calgary and co-author of *Out of Irrelevance: A Socio-Political Introduction to Indian Affairs in Canada*.

Andrew Delisle is chief of the Kahnawake tribe of Quebec and former president of the Confederation of the Indians of Quebec.

Earl Old Person is chief of the Blackfoot tribe of Montana and is active in the National Tribal Chairmen's Association and the National Congress for American Indians.

Sol Sanderson is president of the Federation of Saskatchewan Indians and former chief of the James Smith Band, Saskatchewan.

Del Riley is president of the National Indian Brotherhood and former president of the Union of Ontario Indians.

Sykes Powderface is vice-president of the National Indian Brotherhood; he is a former chief of the Stoney Reserve in Alberta and former president of the Treaty Seven Area Council.

Leroy Little Bear is a professor of Native American Studies at the University of Lethbridge; he is currently consultant to the Department of Indian Affairs and Northern Development on the proposed Indian-government legislation and is the author of numerous reports and publications on aboriginal rights, land claims, and Indian self-government.

Menno Boldt is a professor of Sociology at the University of Lethbridge; an internationally recognized expert on suicide and Indian
mortality, he has been a recipient of the Irwin Stengel Award for
research and publication in the area of suicide prevention and is the
author of numerous articles on Indian leadership, culture, and decision-making.

J. Anthony Long is a professor of Political Science at the University of
Lethbridge and a former dean of Arts and Science; he is the author
of numerous papers and articles on Canadian provincial politics and
the Indian self-government movement.